The Enrollment Effect

LAUREN,

As you Share your message allow your
heart to lead and Step in with
full confidence.

[signature]

479-221-7824

The Enrollment Effect

Form Lasting Relationships
Live Your Ideal Lifestyle
Impact the World

by Tyler Watson

Silver Torch Press
Beverly Hills, CA

The Enrollment Effect: Form Lasting Relationships, Live Your Ideal Lifestyle, Impact the World ©2017 by Tyler Watson

thefreedomcatalyst.com
support@thefreedomcatalyst.coms

Printed in the United States of America.

ISBN: 978-1-942707-66-0
Library of Congress Control Number: 2017955824

 Published by Silver Torch Press
www.SilverTorchPress.com
Jill@SilverTorchPress.com

Information provided in this book is for informational purposes only. This information is NOT intended as a substitute for the advice provided by your physician or other healthcare or mental health provider. Neither the author nor the publisher shall be liable or responsible for any loss or damage allegedly arising from any information or suggestion in this book.

Acknowledgements

I never imagined I would have a book written about anything I did or taught. I do not like writing and could never have gotten this done without a lot of help and influence.

I want to thank Jill Fagan and her amazing team, especially Gwendolyn Weiler, for taking my words and putting them in order and making sense of it all.

I want to thank my wife, Emily, who inspired me to take this journey in the first place and do what I am doing today. For being patient with my weaknesses and embracing my strengths and being my number one mentor and guide.

I also want to acknowledge several of my other mentors over the years who I have learned from, some face-to-face and others through their books and trainings. Ted McGrath, for teaching me about the blueprint and story and helping me realize I had the gift of enrollment all along. Clay Stevens and Hugh Black, for setting examples of how to ask good questions and enrolling me in my vision in a time where I was living beneath my ability.

Raymond Grace, who taught me the power of my mind and how much influence I really have. Bob Proctor, for his way of making things so easy to understand and for his teachings on mindset and vision. Leslie Householder, who helped me imagine something greater than the present amidst fear and doubt. Dr. Anthony James, for teaching me to become a master of my art. Gary Craig, for teaching the world a technique that has influenced and changed my life and that of my family's.

My Aunt Noreen, for setting the example and introducing me to the Law of Attraction. My Mom and Dad, for all they have been through and have taught me over the years. And so many others, who, by their way of living and how they teach, have brought me to where I am today.

Table of Contents

Foreword

If you want to master the most important conversation in business, ENROLLMENT, then Tyler is your guy and this book is your guide.

Today, the world is thirsting for answers to business in a world that is changing rapidly; but one thing still hasn't changed – and that's enrolling customers.

Tyler is a master in explaining step by step how to use the power of stories and how to have authentic conversations that lead to your ideal lifestyle. If you truly want to change the world with the power of the enrollment conversation, then you will love this book. The techniques in this book provide the freedom every entrepreneur is after – freedom of time, freedom of money, and freedom to make the biggest impact possible through the enrollment conversation. I highly recommend you dive in and enjoy all Tyler has to offer, which isn't just a breakthrough in your business, but is a profound breakthrough in how you see your customer and how you show up in this world.

Godspeed,

Ted McGrath
Theater performer, speaker, and best-selling author

INTRODUCTION
The Enrollment Effect

In 2012, I was a massage therapist making between $15-45 an hour. The next year I was newly married, I had a baby on the way, and I was struggling to bring in anything over $1,000 per month. Today, I am earning five to six figures a month teaching message-bearers like you—networkers, trainers, speakers, leaders, healers, those in service-based sales, anyone with a good message—how to share your message, master your stories, and sell your passion in a way that will allow you to start creating five to six figures a month yourself doing what you love most, all while creating more intimate and lasting relationships with those you love. What has made the difference?

I'm going to reveal to you a powerful set of truths that are going to change your life, and the lives of everyone else you meet for the rest of your life. These truths are embodied in what I call The Enrollment Effect.

The Enrollment Effect

The Enrollment Effect becomes active as you define your ideal lifestyle and vision, then find what's stopping or slowing your progress, and commit to learn the skills and master the emotions necessary to become who it takes to make your vision a reality. In essence, you unlock the power to fully master yourself so that you can have, be, and do anything you desire.

The Enrollment Effect embodies many truths and demands, many avenues of action. If you don't commit to mastering both the necessary skills *and* mastering the necessary emotions, you will only receive part of the reward. Perhaps you can still define your ideal vision and lifestyle, but without all of the components in place, you will never be able to be the person capable of claiming them. You can see that pattern with people who win the lottery. If they're not emotionally capable of handling that vision, they'll lose it in a year or two. Or, similarly, when someone finds the right person to be with, but they haven't become the person capable of communicating on that level, the relationship will shortly turn to disaster. That's the shadow of The Enrollment Effect.

As you go through this process of completely enrolling in your own life and tapping in to your massive powers to create, you will not only be qualified, but also have a *burning desire*, to then help others fully enroll in their potential, overcome their addictions, have ideal relationships, and fully live their lives.

We are all being enrolled every day. We are enrolled in waking up early or sleeping late, in making more or less money, into a thriving or a dying relationship, in happiness or in suffering, and in fulfillment or boredom. It's all about how we show up in our lives, and the truths that are governing our actions.

Are you fully enrolled in your truth?

How many lives could you change if fear was a non-issue in your life?

How much money would you be making if you could work exclusively with your ideal clients?

How much more fulfillment would you have if you were living your ideal lifestyle, unbound by worries about money?

How would your relationships be different if you were able to be your best self?

When you decide to enroll with intention, and activate the full power of the truth in your life, you will be able to improve by quantum leaps because you have a solid foundation in place to hold you. By the time you are done reading this book, you will be able to step fully into yourself and unlock your greatest potential to change your life, change the lives around you, and create a movement across the entire planet.

I am going to unfold the mysteries of The Enrollment Effect to you so that you can apply it in your own life in order to:

- Find and monetize your gift, even in your darkest of times.
- Recognize your core truth and how living it is the fastest way to make money.
- See that authentic conversation is the solution to issues pertaining to money, relationships, fulfillment, and even health.
- Embrace what you avoid with faith and determination.
- Overcome feelings of uncertainty and inadequacy.
- Look forward to the sales conversation.
- Form authentic, lasting relationships with clients.
- Connect to those closest to you more intimately.
- Master the art of influence through sharing your truth.
- Rid yourself of judgement and fear.
- Debunk the money objections.
- Inspire others to take action and fully enroll in their lives.
- Naturally find paying clients at networking events.
- Change lives, as opposed to just making an impression.
- Recognize that your greatest struggles and pains up to this point are the very gifts that will help you live a full life.

If you will commit now to do whatever it takes to harness this power, then it's just a matter of time before you are capable of receiving whatever it is you're looking for. This will create a ripple effect in your life, in the lives of others, and throughout the entire world.

However, it's not just about taking action, it's about taking the *right* action. I am going to help navigate you through these three key milestones in your transformation:

1. **Learning how to enroll yourself**. You're going to define your *why*, identify your purpose, and articulate your passion. Once that's clear, you're going to align yourself with those purposes and get rid of the fears that are holding you back from the life you're striving for.

2. **Learning how to enroll others**. You're going to create an irresistible, high-quality package to offer your clients that addresses their unique needs and shows them a step-by-step process on how you are going to change their lives. Your prospects will clearly recognize that every dollar spent with you is a dollar invested into themselves. I will hand you a strategy that leverages the advantages of working smart so that you can achieve your goals and multiply your income twelve times faster.

3. **Learning how to enroll the planet**. You will become so aligned with your message and your passion that you will *be* your message and your passion. Your evolved skills, mindset, and practices will touch all of the relationships in your life, and you will be prepared to help others enroll in a higher cause in all things.

As you move through these milestones, you will quickly recognize that everything has a logical and an emotional link. We're going to combine the two, and we're going to dive into the world of emotions, both yours and your clients'. This may be new territory for you, but I will be your gentle guide the whole way. This is the space where I am most at home and most passionate. I've been learning the art and science of how to help people overcome emotional blocks since I was two years old. I've found what keeps people stuck and mastered how to get people unstuck very quickly. Once upon a time, that was the essence of my career. I worked with people who had been abused, helping them let go of crippling emotions so that they could fully live their lives. Today, I use proven strategies for overcoming blocks in a more universal arena. I am helping people like you achieve your goals up to twelve times faster and live the life you were created for.

Even though we are going to be taking an intimate journey through some big emotions, I assure you that this will be a safe and an amazing ride.

I will also give you a blueprint for your business success. You will receive an exact step-by-step guide to follow—the same blueprint I used to take my business from zero figures up to five and six figures a month in less than a year and a half, with the bulk of that being achieved in a matter of weeks. These are proven strategies that you can duplicate for your own success and create even faster results. Over the past four years, I've invested over $350,000 in learning these techniques and skills from some of the most gifted people I have met. Now, I'm distilling the best parts of my education and handing them to you.

Show Up and Play

In return for all that I am gifting to you, I require that you commit to show up and play the game. I don't want you to just read these pages. I want you to immediately apply the principles I'm going to share. When something inspires you, close the book and write it down. If I give you an exercise, don't continue to read ahead until you've stopped to complete the exercise.

Your success is 100 percent dependent on whether or not you apply what you learn. This book is not meant to just be something that gives you warm fuzzies and hope. My intention is to infuse you with so much passion that you are moved to take the actions that will create immediate change. This isn't a billboard. It's an elevator. If you're going to turn the page and get on, commit to take the ride *up*. This will be one of the most empowering rides you've ever taken—*if* you allow it to be.

I hope you're as excited about taking the ride as I am. I'll see you on the other side.

CHAPTER ONE
Position Yourself for Success

Before we begin, we need to set some expectations and rules. There are two principles which are key to your success: passion and repetition. These are the keys to success in all areas of your life. If I teach you a principle or give you a tool, and you apply it without success, it's not working for one of two reasons: either because you don't have enough passion or because you didn't repeat it enough.

Again, these are proven strategies. I'm not reinventing the wheel here. If something isn't working, recalibrate and try again. Some people try something over and over again, but it doesn't work because in the back of their mind, they're still afraid of success. They lack the passion and confidence required to open new doors. Others are passionate starting out, but they don't follow through with the necessary repetition to keep it going.

I promise you that you're going to run into both tests repeatedly as you position yourself to evolve. There is a threshold to your comfort zone, and it's going to take massive, intentional action to break through that. So, commit to the passion by deciding to repeat the processes that generate the passion. Commit to the repetition by making the decision to continue to move even when it's uncomfortable. This is a must.

Your Musts

Here's the thing about your musts—you make them happen. These are the things that are non-negotiable in your life. Here's my success formula:

wishes ➡ hopes ➡ Wants ➡ NEEDS ➡ MUSTS ➡ DO WHAT IT TAKES

CHAOS   *PEACE*

This formula is governed by three laws: The Law of Attraction, the Law of Gestation, and the Law of Action. When you're in the wishing stage, you're probably living in a state of chaos. The wish comes as a comfort to those negative emotions as you start to fantasize about a better outcome. As you start to wish, this activates the The Law of Attraction, the first of three laws that govern the above formula. However, there's no pull to it until you've reached the wanting stage; at this point it's more like a preview of what you can have.

Then, that wish evolves into a hope for that better outcome. As soon as you allow yourself to think that it could be true, some of the chaos starts to go away. However, it also gets a little more scary because there's a chance you can fail, which creates vulnerability. This is why most people don't get past the wishing stage. As you resist that pull to stay in your chaotic comfort zone, your hope will evolve into wanting. The wanting activates the Law of Gestation, which is about how to cut the waiting time down to its lowest denominator so that you can have what you want as fast as possible. Then, the want evolves into a need. It's as much of a necessity to you as food, water, and air. Here it will naturally move to the state of a must.

Once that wish is elevated to a must, the Law of Action propels you to do whatever it takes to claim it. The Law of Action is the most important of the three laws. You'll find that the more you apply the law of action, the faster the other two laws are going to work for you. You achieve peace when you reach the "must" stage, and nothing is hard when you're at peace. There's no more chaos. When you know that something *must* occur and you start the process of doing what it takes—it doesn't even have to occur yet—you have peace, and then you can easily manifest what you're seeking.

If you're wishing for something now, it's going to stay a wish indefinitely unless you act on that wish with an outside force to evolve it into a must. You can do this with anything. If you wish you could create $30,000 in a month (or $100,000 or $500,000—whatever the number is for you), you can take that wish and transform it into a must. Once it hits that level, it's as important as air, and you'll automatically do what it takes. You will see opportunities you didn't see before. You will take actions you didn't think you were capable of taking before. It's like the stories we hear of superhuman strength—mothers lifting cars off of their children. Did they wish they could do it? No. They did it because it HAD to be done. The how is irrelevant at that point. The outcome is all that matters.

Your challenge is to learn how to evolve your wishes into musts. As you are passionate about this truth, and as you leverage repetition in practicing the strategies, you'll be able to shorten that process over time.

The Black Stranger

In my life, I've had an uncanny ability to do whatever it takes and quickly evolve my wishes into musts, regardless of the cost or what fears come up. I'm grateful for that. I believe part of this ability is due to my ancestry—specifically, inherited from my Danish Viking ancestor, The Black Stranger.

It was announced that there would be a race to a specific part of Ireland, and the first person who touched the land would get to rule over it as king. My ancestor decided that he was going to win. The race began, and he was driven to succeed. However, in spite of his determination, he started to fall behind. He was losing. Inside, however, he *knew* that nothing was going to keep him from winning. He finally saw land and pushed himself as hard as he could. But as he was pulling up close to the island, he

saw another ship even closer. The other captain was going to land there first. So, my ancestor lifted his battle axe and brought it down hard, chopping off his left hand. He then threw it at the island so that he would be officially the first person to touch the land.

He became King.

I like to share this story any time I'm talking to people who say they tried so hard and did everything possible, but still failed. This story represents so much. My ancestor knew, more than anything, that he was willing to go beyond the normal parameters of "everything possible". Losing just was not an option. There was no chance he was not going to make it, even if all logic defied him, because it was a must. He decided that was what he was going to do, and he did whatever it took.

So, let this be a lesson to you as you are growing your business and trying to be the person capable of claiming your vision. If you believe you've tried your hardest, then try *his* hardest. No, I'm not suggesting that you cut off parts of your body. However, I am insisting that you have to think outside the box and really push yourself—do *whatever* it takes, as long as it's legal, ethical, moral, fun, and intelligent. If you've exhausted your skill set, then learn a new one. Be willing to face and to overcome all your fears, no matter the pain. When something challenging comes up, instead of backing down, think of my ancestor, The Black Stranger[1], who was willing to do whatever it took to conquer that section of land. When he realized that his current skills came up short to give him victory, he improvised new ones.

Be a 100 Percenter

Does this make you feel empowered? Or do you feel anxious and overwhelmed? This would be a good time to take an inventory of where you are. Generally, I find that there are three types of people:

- The 30 percenters: These are the people you teach, but they only listen. They don't do anything. They learn the strategies and the templates and the breakthroughs, but they don't apply them. (I used to work almost exclusively with this group of people because I had what I call "Savioritis." I'll talk more about that later.)

- The 60 percenters: These people will do about half of what you teach them, and they will get half the results. They're usually happy and complacent with the results they have, but they're not reaching their full potential.

---

[1] When we're talking about the generational stuff, people are usually referencing the generational negative things they've inherited. However, it's powerful, when you're able to start, to honor your past and all the *good* things you've inherited. This unlocks the power of those gifts so that they can fuel your future. So, I share this story to inspire you to honor the generations before you, and to take the good qualities you've been given and use them.

- The 100 percenters: These people govern their lives by the law of action. They're the doers. They learn new things then immediately apply them. They not only get the results they desire, but they're moving with so much momentum when they get there that they naturally go above and beyond. These are the extra milers and the over-achievers.

What kind of person are you? If you're feeling anxious, then your comfort zone may be in the 30 or 60 percenter camp. However, the beauty is that you get to decide who you are going to be, and where you are going to go. Decide now to be a 100 percenter. Start becoming different so you can be around and attract different people. If you feel plagued by limiting beliefs at this point, just keep riding that elevator. We're going to get to the floor where we rid you of those fears soon. Just stay with me.

Right now, I need you to decide to be a 100 percenter because that's what it's going to take for you to make the impact you want to. You have a message the planet needs. Whether you know your message or are still trying to find it, you are the only bearer of this message. If you fall short of your goals, there is no one else to pass the torch to. It is you, or it is no one. There are people whose lives are waiting to be changed by what you have to offer. Regardless of how many people are doing something similar to you, you have a unique voice and energy that certain people are waiting, and some even praying, for. You have a responsibility to them. As you hold yourself to the standard of 100 percent, you are qualified to raise others to their 100 percent.

As a 100 percenter, you are positioned to use this book to build an infrastructure and create a lifestyle-friendly business that will impact thousands, if not hundreds of thousands, of people with twelve times the speed. I hire mentors and get into programs, not because I don't think I can succeed otherwise, but because I want to succeed that much faster. The 30 percenters aren't like that. Their mentality is, "Save me! Do it for me!" They're so desperate that they are going to grab on to you and pull you under with them. You don't want to be that person; and you don't want to work with people like that. True success is when you teach a person to fish, as opposed to giving them a fish over and over again.

Accountability

Here we are at the very beginning, and I've already required quite a bit of you. Now it's time that you require something of yourself. Require yourself to stay accountable for the commitments to action you've made. Your success or failure is up to you. I'm not there to coach you through this in person. Before you move on from here, write down the amount of time you're going to allot, and at what hour you're going to commit, to apply these principles each day. Treat this as seriously as a college-level business class, if not more seriously.

People invest hundreds of thousands of dollars and four years of their lives to go to a college they don't care about or into a major they aren't sure about. Then they graduate and get a part-time job doing something completely different. I earned a bachelor's of science degree in Biology Pre-Med. People ask me why I have it, and I say, "To hang on my wall," but I don't even do that with it! If we are willing to spend that much time and money on something with such a small guarantee of ROI, how can we purchase a mentoring package or buy a book that can unlock our potential and then fail to make it a top priority? You have a degree in life experiences. Use it. Study and apply things that pertain to you and your mission or cause.

What we're doing together right now is arguably more important than that college degree you paid for because this is going to pay you back with interest. If I can help you create wealth doing what you love while being authentic in your relationships, what's that worth to you? Think about it. Thriving in your relationships, mastering the communication process, eliminating your limiting beliefs around money, and actually looking forward to that money conversation with your high-end clients. If you want to position yourself to enroll higher paying clients, from two thousand dollar packages all the way up to sixty thousand dollars and beyond, you've got to understand that the details matter. What you're doing is a top priority. So, value yourself enough right now to take out your calendar and schedule in time to go through the steps I'm going to give you.

If you're the kind of person who enrolls into a program and doesn't get value out of it, it's because you haven't held yourself accountable, and you don't value yourself as much as you should. I know because I used to be that person. Once I changed that mindset and committed to being a 100 percenter and holding myself accountable, everything changed.

My Story

When I was 12 years old, my dad sat me down, looked me in the eyes, and said, "Tyler, your mom and I are getting a divorce." In that moment, I took on the subconscious belief that I wasn't good enough and it was all my fault. I became an overachiever, always trying to earn this elusive love I didn't feel I was worthy of. My mom went through three more divorces and my dad another, giving me proof that I. was destined to fail at marriage, business, and life. However, I put on a happy face because I believed I had to be perfect.

I felt like I had to fix everything for everyone and was eager to try. My mom would tell me to go tell my dad this, and then

14

my dad would tell me to tell my mom that, and round and round we'd go. I did this for years until I learned to hate communicating. I was unable to share what was really going on inside of me and unsure of who or what to believe. Don't get me wrong, my parents did an amazing job at raising me, and I'm blessed to have them. However, one thing I felt like I missed out on was feeling understood. So, I turned to something that I thought could understand me—pornography, the destroyer of all that is pure and good. How twisted, right? I turned to the very thing that was guaranteed to stop my success. I became depressed and struggled with thoughts of suicide. I didn't feel like I had any value at all and actually believed that the people I loved would be better off if I didn't exist. I wasn't even sure if they would care or notice that I was gone.

This continued for years until I decided to change. I got cleaned up and left for a two-year service mission in Mexico for my church, The Church of Jesus Christ of Latter-day Saints. Upon returning and graduating college, I became a Massage therapist. I knew I had a gift that could really help people and change lives, but I believed I didn't deserve to be paid what I was worth and continued to struggle with addiction. I was making between $15-45 an hour as a massage therapist, and I was lucky to work a few hours a week. At the time, I felt that was pretty good, but I wasn't attracting the right clientele. I was finding people who didn't have any money, and I found myself always giving my gift away for free.

Then I realized that I needed money to live life more fully. I needed to eat. I needed to keep my power on. I needed to keep my car insured. I was in a rut. I could see the rut. But I couldn't see a way out. My life was in chaos, and I was tired of fighting all of these internal battles. I knew I needed to change for good. I tuned in to my Higher Power, seeking guidance, and I had a distinct thought come to my mind and my heart, which was that

I needed to learn about money—how to create it, receive it, manage it, keep it, and how to bless others with it. That was a huge moment of change for my life because I was led to change careers and to become a mentor. I quit my job and left my clinic, even though I was financially struggling and just barely married. This became a must for me. I had no choice but to make this happen.

With a pregnant wife back home and me bringing in less than $1,000 a month, I went out and talked to over twenty different company leaders about how to change their lives and gain success. I look like I'm sixteen years old, so I can imagine what that was like for them. The first one said no. The second one said no. I went from one to the next, to the next, to the next, until twenty-six leaders had told me no. I can tell you from experience that when people aren't valuing your message the way you'd like them to, and if you're not getting paid what you're worth, it's not a good place in which to be. I felt completely demoralized and discouraged. I went back to my car and sat there crying, thinking if I could just take a nap, it would be better when I woke up. I went to sleep, but things were the same when I awoke.

At that moment, I received an email about a webinar that would teach me about being authentic and using money to help people. It was in line with my immediate goals. It looked like a door sent by my Higher Power. I signed up for it right then and there.

But there was a problem.

The program being offered on the free webinar required an investment of $1997. I only had $600 in my bank account. I was afraid to invest, as I had already borrowed $5400 the month before for a program that hadn't gotten the results I wanted. I knew I needed to take action again but I was even more afraid of continuing to live in a state of chaos. Right then, I *chose* a different path, regardless of what I would have to go through to get there. It became a must. In that moment, I had an overwhelming feeling of peace. I knew this was the key to sharing my message, and I would do whatever it took to make this happen. I found a way and invested.

The next week, using the principles I'm going to teach you in this book, I created $6,400 in one week, doing exactly what I loved most. The next month, I made more than $10,000. The next month, I made more than $15,000. The trend continued until I was earning more than $35,000 per month—hitting a high of $240,000 in one month—sharing my message with others. The numbers are consistent and continue to climb. The reason for this is simple. I didn't just *invest* into that webinar. I took it to heart and immediately *applied* the principles. I valued myself enough to make the investment of funds and then honor that with the investment of my time and passion. As soon as I started to invest in myself, I was able to take my life stories and combine them with the necessary skills to get myself out of bondage and help other people do the same.

That wasn't the last time I invested into myself and my education, nor was it the least expensive investment I've made—not by a long shot. I've invested over $340,000 into myself over the past 4 years, learning the strategies that I'm sharing with you now. Today, I am delivering much more impact getting paid what I'm earning now compared to when I was getting paid $15 an hour as a Massage therapist. I love teaching, meeting new people, and traveling the world. I spend my time mentoring people like you who have messages and gifts to share, and who are making a change on our planet. I also spend more time on vacations. I do a week-long vacation every two to three months, and mini vacations all the time. I even went a time working only three days a week to test these principles of abundance, and they continued to work for me. Today, I'm still me. I'm just a better me.

The Cost of Inaction

I can give you a number to quantify the dollar value of what I've spent learning these principles. I can even give you a number to quantify the dollar value of what I have earned as a result. However, what would it have cost me if I didn't make this change? I was struggling to make ends meet. I didn't understand how money worked, how people invested in things, or how to create wealth. I struggled through my emotions with addictions like pornography that ate me up inside. The quality of my life was dictated by my fears and limiting beliefs. I had a fear of being judged. I was discouraged by my previous failures. I was a slave to money, always framing my life choices and opportunities around whether or not I had it. Staying in that place came with a price—to me, my relationships, the people I had a responsibility to serve, and the entire planet.

It's the same for you. There is a direct cost to you and those you are responsible to serve when you stay in the same, comfortable place day after day. What is it costing *you* to stay the same? What is the cost of inaction in your life?

Take Immediate Action

Now, get a pen and a piece of paper and take immediate action to change your life. We are going to take actions throughout this book so the Law of Action can start to mold your life from this moment forward.

Right now, write down the answer to this question:
What is the cost to staying where you are?

Now I want you to really tune in and ask yourself the following questions and write down the first number that comes into your head.

What is the cost this year? Over the next three years? Five years? A lifetime?

When I first did this exercise, the answer was "millions." I didn't want to write it down because I didn't want to face what was real. However, I'm asking you to write it down, whatever that number is, because you need to get present to this. As you get present to what it's costing you, you will be able to help your clients see what it's costing them, too.

In addition to money, some of the costs you're incurring are:

- Having to work harder than you need to, but without the desired results.
- Fear, frustration, and feeling overwhelmed.
- The cost of investing money in personal development, yet not creating money back.
- Stress on your relationships. It's hard for you to be present with the ones you love when you're absorbed by money problems or fear.

So, choose action. Move into the following pages knowing that you are going to get value out of them, knowing what you want to achieve, and having expectations for yourself. Do this one bite, one chunk, at a time because you're committed to changing the world—one person at a time.

CHAPTER TWO
Break Free

In order to prime you to share your message, first we need to prime the message bearer. You. The Enrollment Effect requires that you master the emotions necessary to become who it takes to make your vision a reality.

The French writer Alexandre Dumas said, "A person who doubts himself is like a man who would enlist in the ranks of his enemies and bear arms against himself. He makes his failure certain by himself, being the first person to be convinced of it." When you go to share your message, what is it that tends to stop you? Be vulnerable and write that down. When you are able to become aware of that, sometimes that alone is the transformation you need. If you can recognize the blocks that keep you from doing what you know is right, then you'll be able to see those same blocks in your clients, and you'll be able to help them. As intimate as your fears and blocks feel to you, they are never original.

Some of the blocks I had to work through were:

- Not knowing how to communicate my message effectively.
- Feeling underqualified to share my message.
- Feeling crippled when it came to asking clients for money.
- Feeling too "sales-y".

- Trying to do everything myself and feeling afraid to ask for or invest in help.
- Feeling unable to build a team that can duplicate results.

These are just some of the things that kept me from moving forward. I couldn't fix them until I was aware of them. It's vital that you recognize the beliefs and feelings that are blocking you because what you fear is a reflection of what you face. You may resist or disagree with what I am going to say next, but it's true. If your clients say they don't have money, it's a reflection of the money mindset inside of you. If they say they don't have time, or they aren't sure they are interested, that's a reflection of what's going on inside of you. I hope you'll be open enough to let that sink in. As you master yourself, you will be able to help others do the same.

People often feel so defined by their limitations that they can't separate them from who they are. For instance, maybe you identify as someone who can't sell because you are a shy introvert. I used to be that person. I believed I was an introvert and that it was scary for me to talk to people, so it was. Growing up, I was one of those kids who would sit in class and wouldn't talk to anyone because I was scared of people. I was the kid who would sit on the bus and look out the window, hoping I would just fall asleep, or I would wait until I got home to talk to anyone. That's how introverted I was. I had only one friend.

It wasn't until I was in the seventh grade that I tried to change my life because I didn't want to be that way anymore. I don't believe that my circumstances dictate who I am. So, when I felt that resistance, I thought, "Why am I scared to talk to people? Why can't I be good friends with these people? Is that something that you're just born with?" I didn't want to believe that. I didn't want to believe that I was bound to be the same for the rest of my life. I wanted to believe I was a creator and that I could change my results and my experiences. I started changing. If a fear came up, I would address it instead of shutting down.

These tools I'm giving you are to help you change, too. If you're getting a consistent undesirable result in any area of your life right now, take note of it, but do not be a slave to that result. If you have a fear, recognize it, and then start to change it. It's a journey. It's not a one-night fix. Even after all the changes I made as a teenager, I was still scared to death to share my message as an adult because I tied my message to my personal value and who I am as a human being. The problem is that I didn't know who I was. When I went to share my message and got rejected, I took it personally, as if it was me being rejected. In time, I changed that to realize that I was sharing my message to find specific people—people who were already dedicated to change. As I started shifting my mindset, I was able to attract higher paying customers who were more motivated. Your message alone is not enough to get the results you want. Who you are inside attracts certain people to you.

Choose to Break Free

Changing your mindset and becoming more confident starts with making a choice. Everything does. People trapped in a victim mentality choose to be there. They choose to become a victim of their circumstances instead of stepping up to the plate and doing something about them. This goes both ways. You also get to choose to break free. It's a decision that is a *must*. You are no longer going to wait for life to happen *to* you. You are going to make it happen *for* you.

Don't allow yourself to drown in excuses of why you aren't getting the results you want. "It's money. It's the government. It's how I was raised. It's my health. I tried, and it didn't work."

No! You are damming, or rather damning yourself by believing these lies. A dam stops the action and the flow. If you aren't getting the results you want, it's because you've already been dammed up.

Unblock this living Hell, because that's what it is.

Damnation is simply the inability to change. If you're stuck getting the same results, it's because you haven't decided to change. Once you decide, the how will come. When you are finally so fed up that getting unstuck becomes a must, you figure it out.

You can't change the government, or a spouse, or the outside world. However, you can change your thoughts, your emotions, and your reactions. When you change, your relationships change. When you change, your income changes. When you change, your happiness changes. Right now, I'm calling you out. Stop being a slave. It's time to break those chains and live a higher mission—the mission your Higher Power has called you to live. You will never discover this mission until you are ready. When you are ready, the walls will be lifted, and the path will be visible. You will no longer be living in your own Hell. You will be un-damned, and you will find your passion, your money, your thriving relationships—the life that you know you were created to live.

It starts with a choice. Choose right now to be a creator. Today. Not tomorrow, or on Monday, or in the new year. Now. Forget all the junk around you that teaches you that you are supposed to be a certain way. I decided I was going to be a catalyst for freedom and decided to break those chains and no longer be a slave to the things around me. I decided to listen to the voice of my Higher Power. Progress may come in increments, but the decision to change happens right now.

$E=mc^2$

I'm going to give you an equation that is going to completely alter your ability to get the results you want. It was founded by Einstein himself. This is an eternal principle that has lasted forever and will continue to last. It makes up the universe—including our successes and our failures. If you can get this principle, it will change your life. When I first learned it, I finally realized why my money wasn't where I wanted it to be, why my relationships were eluding me, and why I wasn't attracting high-paying clients. If I can get you to see, as I'm seeing, and visualize a bigger perspective; then as you go to make your impact and enroll clients, you'll be able to treat them differently and do things on a bigger level.

This is important, so I need you to commit to focus on this. If you can get this principle, it will change your life. Clear all of your distractions and get present. You can quickly ground yourself by taking a minute to take some deep breaths in and releasing them.

Are you ready?

Write down this equation: $E=mc^2$. This is Einstein's law of relativity. Everything I'm going to teach you is based on this law. To better understand this, let's break down the pieces of the equation.

The "E" stands for "energy." The Law of Conservation states that energy can neither be created nor destroyed; it can only be transformed from one form to another. This is important.

The "m" stands for "mass." Basically, the mass of an object is a measure of the number of atoms in it—or in other words, a measurement of matter. What is matter? Everything that exists. That means that everything has a mass, and is therefore a variable in this equation. Even your thoughts. In your brain, when you have an idea, there are things that are firing—protons, electrons, quarks—which create a process that can be measured. Think of an EEG, which measures brain activity.

The "c" represents the speed of light. The speed of light is constant and, for our purposes, all we need to recognize is that it's really fast. So, what is energy? Energy is mass sped up really fast.

From the equation, we know that if you increase the numerical value of energy, it increases the numerical value of mass. If you increase the numerical value of mass, it increases the numerical value of energy. What does this have to do with anything? Hopefully some lightbulbs are starting to turn on.

If you want to increase the mass of something in your life, you need to increase the energy you're putting in. If you want to increase the mass of the money in your life, increase the energy you're putting into it. Whether or not you're in a broken relationship is a measure of the amount of energy being put into it. Your health, and whether or not you have dis-ease or are overweight, is a representation of the energy inside of you. Scientifically, there is a direct cause-and-effect relationship between energy and what is manifest, or mass.

You can change the numerical values in this equation at any time. This means that you can change everything fast. If you change the energy around your life, what you think, and how you live, the manifestations, or mass, of your life is also going to change.

For example, if I'm trying to create $30,000 a month, and I'm not creating it, I must look at the energy and ask, "What's stopping this result from manifesting? What negative actions and thoughts do I constantly do or think that take up precious energy? What amount of energy is required to move the needle to the mass value I want?"

The energy we're going to target here is the energy of our thoughts. Let's say you have a positive thought that you want to create $30,000 this month. You hold that positive energy for a millisecond before it's neutralized by negative thoughts like, "It's too hard. You'd have to pay too many taxes." In this event, the best-case scenario is that the net energy being invested becomes zero, but in reality, it's usually in the negative. You don't feel neutral about the idea of making $30,000 in a month; you feel defeated, upset, and negative about it. It's easy to tell what's going on in people's lives by measuring the results they're getting. If you aren't where you want to be, you're allowing your surroundings and your thoughts to reduce your energy to the point that it's either completely ineffective (the best-case scenario), or sabotaging you (which is more likely).

What does it take to change?

Look at the diagram on the next page. All of us have a threshold where we have set limits for our energy levels. It exists because we're mortal, and setting limits is human nature. It's because of your parents, the way you were raised, what you ate for lunch, and because of everything else you've done in your life. It's simply the programs that you have instilled since childhood. When you're born, that line isn't there. You naturally put it there as you start to recognize danger and withdraw to safety. Once it's there, the moment you go to change something, it has to pass through the threshold under which everything is safe. This triggers the sense of danger. I've seen this many times. People start to work on increasing the mass of their income. They start at easy and go up and up and up—and as soon as they get to that threshold and pass over it, they say, "I'm going to create $20,000 this month." They put in the effort and do what has to be done. Until they freak out.

Chaos happens, and something breaks down, or limiting beliefs about money cause emotional havoc, or a relationship goes

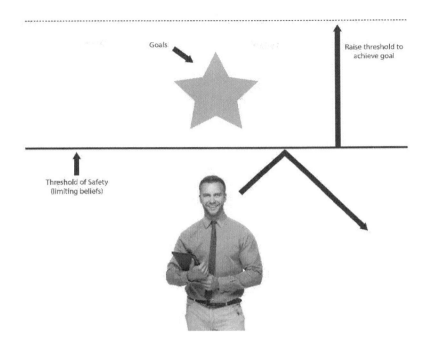

bad. Whatever it is, something happens to bring you back below the threshold where you are back to "safe." This can happen to you over and over again, for years. I know people who've been living this way for twenty to forty years. Either they can't make more money, they are repeating the same crappy relationships, or they never lose the weight. Whatever it is, they are always blaming other outside circumstances. They don't realize they have this threshold, and that if they just raised their energy through personal development, letting go of negative thoughts and habits, increasing the work value, or learning the necessary skills, everything would change. Otherwise, chaos is going to happen in your life. As your energy goes up, your mass also has to go up, which is sometimes scary because it's new. So you backtrack. Less energy, less mass—less responsibility, less room for failure or pain. The equation equals back out.

This next diagram shows you where your thoughts come in to play. Your thoughts create your emotions, which create your actions (these three comprising your energy), which produces your results (your mass). The threshold is a wall between your energy and your mass. The fastest way to get through that threshold and create the mass you're aiming for is to master your thoughts and emotions.

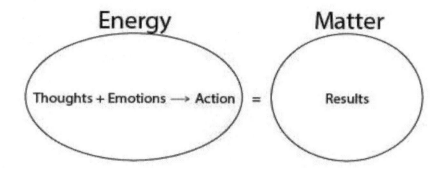

This means you commit to take the actions that you know will lead to your desired results, regardless of what's going on with your thoughts and your emotions. This commitment alone will immediately start to raise your energy. Do not allow your thoughts and emotions to dictate your actions. Most people do this. The result is that success is not sustained. In marriage, peo-ple fall out of love, so they divorce; but they stopped loving each other because they stopped taking the necessary actions to maintain that result. In business, people stop doing strategy calls because they believe they are introverts and the conversations are awkward. This leads to thoughts that they *can't* do strategy sessions. They drop their energy, and they go back to safe.

In the movie *Fireproof*, the main character goes on a forty-day program to change his marriage. After just a few days, he's discouraged and wants to quit. His father encourages him to keep his forty-day commitment to act, regardless of how he's feeling. He does, and things end predictably well for the character. The point is that he wanted to quit after just a few days. He was coming up against that threshold. You, too, are guaranteed to come up against that threshold. It's a test. Are you going to keep going?

If you continue to push and invest the requisite amount of energy by continuing to have those awkward conversations, releasing your negative emotions, doing the strategy calls, staying accountable, and measuring your goals—if you keep making the investment, the threshold has to change. Just keep doing it. Those scary thoughts will still come, and you can release them, or you can flat out say, "Thanks for telling me, but I don't need you anymore. I'm done with you." Acknowledge the thought, and let it go. Then you keep on moving, acting, and doing. If you get to a point where you feel your energy drop, a quick way to get it back up is speaking. This is why affirmations and declarations work so well. Everything will change as you stay committed to act. Identify the one thing that scares you, and go do it anyway.

When I first started, I knew this principle, and I was still scared. However, I went out and knocked on ten doors. My thoughts and emotions were going everywhere. "What are you doing? This is a waste of time. You won't succeed." I didn't care what my thoughts and emotions did. I was going to keep doing what I was doing, even though the first few people didn't want to work with this punk kid who looked like he was twelve or talk to him about changing their lives. I consciously decided that I wasn't going to let my actions be dictated by my fears or my negative thoughts. I went and went and went. By the time I knocked on the tenth door and spoke to my tenth person, no one had invested in me. However, I had raised my threshold by a huge margin. I proved to myself that I could do it.

I went and had a pep talk with myself out in the woods. I was still scared and never wanted to do it again. But the next day, I went back at it. I kept going. That continued effort lead to selling my first package. I made $1,500. I wanted to wet myself. That result, that mass, was a direct result of having done so much to change my energy. It was a must for me. I was committed to do anything to change my results. From there, my results continued getting bigger until now I'm consistently making five to six figures each month.

It's universally true that raising your energy is going to simultaneously raise your mass and move your threshold higher and higher. However, it's also true that once you push through that threshold, there's going to be some pushback and a series of tests. Chaos is going to try to intimidate you back to safety. In the next two chapters, I'm going to teach you the vital principles and techniques you need in order to maintain your ground so you can successfully start making shifts right now.

Take Immediate Action

Before you move on, though, I want you to take a minute and shift your direction for immediate change.

First, take a deep breath and slowly let it out so that you can get re-grounded and tap in to your intuition and Higher Power. Take another deep breath in, and slowly let it out.

Once you are still enough to really listen, ask yourself what one action you need to take right now to start increasing your mass. Stay centered and present as the answer forms in your heart and mind. It is probably the action that most scares you. Ask yourself what area of your life needs this movement, whether it's your relationships, finances, health—whatever it is. Maybe you have to talk to someone you've been avoiding, or set a goal for a certain number of strategy sessions, or quit eating those cheeseburgers and fries. Just pick one action. Be specific.

Once you identify what you need to do, write it down. You'll immediately feel that push against your threshold. Accept that and commit to move forward anyway. Remember, this is a must now. The message you carry is too important for you to stay in your safety zone. Instead, stretch beyond your threshold and give it the room it needs to change lives—and to change the planet.

CHAPTER THREE
Fight the Real Battle

In order to maintain any ground you gain, you need to understand the Principle of Flow, which states: As you put things in, things have to come out. Everything I'm going to teach you will come back to this. This is a simple, universal principle. For example, think of food. What goes in also has to come out, either as energy or as waste. What if we didn't have a way to let things out? If you drank water and didn't have a way to sweat or urinate it out, you'd just continue to swell until you popped. Similarly, as I teach you how to put in good things—doing your declarations and vision boards, making commitments to act, writing your story, creating packages—these things are not just taking up empty space. You have to make space for them.

You are already filled with a lifetime of habits, beliefs, stories, and ideas. If we only put new things in, and we don't utilize the tools to release the old, what's going to happen? You're going to expand and get so packed that you explode or shut down. You'll start blowing up at everybody or start to feel depressed as you hit maximum emotional capacity. Perhaps you have experienced this already. This is why every single tool I'm going to give you is going to do one of two things. It is going to put something in or let something out. Fortunately, you receive an upgraded cup as you apply The Enrollment Effect in your life and grow in your skill and emotional capacity. You will have the ability to hold more as you expand yourself. However, this does not negate the need for flow

Self-development programs often skip this vital step. Imagine walking into your kitchen after a Super Bowl party. The sink is full of dishes, there's food spattered on the stove, and the table is covered with dirty paper plates and cups still half-filled with soda. You look around at the mess, and you want to improve the way it looks and feels. So, you go to the store and buy a bouquet of wildflowers. The colors are vibrant, and they smell amazing. You go home, put them in a vase, and then place them right in the middle of your table. Your spouse comes home later and says, "We need to clean up!"

You just smile and say, "Honey, I already fixed the problem."

"What do you mean you fixed the problem? Don't you see the dishes and the mess and the trash everywhere?"

"Don't you see the flowers?"

Obviously, you have to do more than bring home flowers. Even though they are beautiful and they smell good, you have to create an appropriate space for them to do their job. Similarly, going through self-development programs may make deposits into you, but you still need to do some cleaning up and putting away in order for new ideas to make their maximum impact on your life.

It's a common misconception to think that acknowledging the negatives is a bad thing. However, that's the equivalent of deciding not to acknowledge the weeds in your garden in order to make it more beautiful. That doesn't make sense. If you want your garden to be beautiful, you have to remove the weeds. I'm not suggesting that you go yell at everyone in order to release anger and frustration. That's just going to multiply the negatives on our planet. However, there are effective and positive ways to release them, and I'm going to share one of the easiest and most powerful ways to do that in just a minute. As you release the negatives in your life, you maximize the positive net worth of your energy investment, which is going to create more results, or mass. $E=mc^2$.

Fix Your Flats

Imagine you're in a race car. You're flying around the track at 150 mph. All of a sudden, the wheel starts shaking. What do you do? Some drivers are going to floor it and go faster (we'll talk about that in a minute). However, the common-sense move is to get a good grip on the wheel, brake to slow down, and pull off into the pit stop. Your team checks your tires and sees that you have a bad tire. They take it off and put on a new one. Then you kick it into gear and take off, going twice as fast as before.

Now, the problem with most people is that they're driving down the road of life, and all of a sudden, their tires and foundation get a little shaky. Instead of stopping and pulling over to fix the flat, or the wobbly tire, they just go faster, thinking, "Maybe if I just speed up, no one will notice the tire!" They speed up, and the shaking gets worse until the tire suddenly explodes. They're still driving, and by now that rim is digging into the concrete. They're saying, "Oh, I got it, I got it. I'm fine." They're putting on a mask of positive thinking to prove that they're good enough. "I can do this, I can do this!"

All of a sudden, the back tire goes out, too. Boom! They're waving off the crew, "No, it's OK, it's OK. I'm fine. I'm thinking positive thoughts. Nothing negative happens in my life. I focus on the positive, and I'm a positive person." They just keep going. Then the next tire falls off. Then the next. They come to a grinding halt, burnt out, frustrated, tired, and their engine's on fire. This ruins the rest of their life.

In order to reach your peak potential, you need to fix your flat tires—the negative emotions that are sabotaging your momentum. We aren't going to ignore the flat tire or try to use a positive attitude to fix it. Instead, we are going to focus on it so that we can see it in every detail. We aren't just going to gloss over it. We are going to get our hands dirty and call it by name. You can't change the flat without acknowledging it. You can't put a new tire on without first handling the old one and taking it off.

What are the flat tires in your life? It's time to fix them so you can hit your optimum speed and start changing lives—beginning with your own.

I have coached hundreds of people through this and have gotten incredible results, from helping people create money to helping people diffuse the emotional effects of abuse so they can live their lives again as whole people. Some real examples include:

John, who had plenty financially, but who was physically and emotionally overdrawn. He has two kids and a lovely wife, but he struggled with feelings of low self-value and worth. His weight climbed to over 350 pounds, and he was depressed. He believed he wasn't able to provide any value to other people. He didn't feel he was a good provider for his family emotionally or physically. He felt as if people were always taking advantage of him. His life had stalled out, and he was stuck in a cycle of misery. He came to a point where he was finally ready to change. After battling the outside world for years—other people, his wife, and all of the other factors over which he had no control—I was able to help him finally see where the real battle was. When he learned and applied the necessary principles and strategies, everything turned around. He immediately started engaging people on a higher level—his wife, his children, his clients, everyone. He used the same techniques I'm going to give you to save his marriage and completely turn himself around emotionally, which positioned him to turn *everything* around.

Then there's Anne, who had been hurt and abused by an older brother growing up. At the time she and I met, she couldn't even receive a hug or a kiss from her little boy. As soon as he started to embrace her, she would lock up in fear. She went on a journey to figure out what was stopping her from engaging in a more fulfilling relationship with her child. I taught her the same core principles and techniques I'm going to teach you, which helped her see where the real battle was. She immediately went home that day and applied these tools. She embraced her son, and when he gave her a kiss, she was flooded with the warm emotions she'd been longing to feel. She hadn't felt that way in ten years.

There's Galen, an avid tennis player whose knee started hurting every time he played. I told him that when he discovered the real battle, the pain would be reduced. He was very skeptical. But he went through it and learned how to shift—not just emotions, but pain. He went through this process and was still skeptical, thinking it was just something that had taken his mind off the pain. However, he soon realized that the pain was gone. It had vanished. He went from a non-believer to a believer that fast. Now, every time that pain starts creeping back in, he can immediately get to the root cause and diffuse it. (If you don't get to the root cause, things can return. We'll touch more on that later.)

The tools I'm about to give you work, regardless of what situation you're in—whether it's a relationship, finances, or any other area of your life. If there's any goal that you haven't yet achieved, and you feel you should have, it's because you have hidden, underlying negative emotions inhibiting your success. I'm going show you how to easily, quickly and, more important, effectively remove those blocks.

The Foundation

First, you need to understand that the real battle you're fighting is in your heart and mind—*not* other people. John felt the real battle was with his spouse and other people. However, once he fought the battle in his heart and mind, all of his other relationships improved. Once he felt worthy of love, he felt his wife's love. Once he felt worthy to receive, he no longer felt as if people were only taking from him and never giving back.

I'm going to drill this into your mind over and over again: the real battle is in your heart and in your mind. In your heart, you have emotions. In your mind, you have thoughts. The real battle is with your emotions and your thoughts. This leads us to the fact that all negative emotions come from fighting the wrong battle. You're probably thinking, "Wait. *All* negative emotions?" Yes. All negative emotions. For example, think of Anne. She had been hurt in the past by her brother and been through some terrible experiences of abuse. She felt her brother was the enemy. Right now, you probably agree with that.

No.

The real battle was in her own head and her own heart. That's where she carried the burdens of hate, disgust, and fear. It wasn't her brother she'd been fighting her whole life. She was literally fighting those negative emotions she associated with her brother and his abuse. She couldn't let go of them because she didn't know how and didn't have the tools. Her past abuse stayed present in her life because of the emotions and the thoughts that were stuck inside of her. However, once she identified the real battle and had the tools to fight it, she was able to eliminate all negative emotions from that experience. She was finally free.

Are you ready to eliminate the burden of negative emotions in your life? Have you been fighting some misplaced battles? If you're honest with yourself, you know you have. In fact, I guarantee you are right now, even if haven't identified them yet. If someone pulls out in front of you and you get mad at the other driver, you're fighting the wrong battle. If someone says something to you and it triggers an emotion of disgust or hatred, you're fighting the wrong battle. If you feel worthless or not valuable, you're fighting the wrong battle. If you've been trying to make a certain amount of money but can't seem to break through to the next level, you're fighting the wrong battle.

Once you can see this is true, you can finally be free. My goal is to help you open your eyes so you can see more clearly and fight the real battle, which is in your heart and in your mind— and eventually get to a place where you no longer have to fight a battle at all because of who you are and how you show up. This is the foundation of all success.

The Science

There's a simple biological process that causes these thoughts and emotions to get stuck. You don't need to understand it in order to know how to get them unstuck, but I find it helps to share it anyway in order to help your left brain make sense of the technique I'm going to share with you.

We all have these things called neurons inside of our brain. The neuron is what receives and sends signals. Your thoughts come in through your brain, go through a dendrite, then into the cell body. This sends another signal out of what's called an axon, which initiates a chain reaction of chemicals and electrical signals. This is the biological process that makes up who we are—what we do, how we act, how we think, how we breathe— everything we do stems from these little neurons.

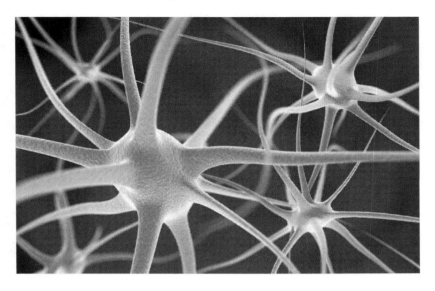

When a thought, or electrical signal, is leaving the neuron, it has to jump this gap called a synapse before it gets into the myelin sheathes and into the ends of the axon and into the next neuron. This synapse is the actual battleground we're going to address. [image of blown up synapse] The synapse is filled with neurotransmitters. If your ducks are in a row, and things are working properly, the signal should come across and pass easily from neuron to neuron and on throughout your body to give you various signals and experiences.

However, emotions will make that signal leave an impression in the neurotransmitters, which essentially means that the emotion gets stuck there. Emotions, by definition, are a series of chemicals and chemical reactions inside of you. However, when negative emotions leave an impression, it fills the neuro gap with imprinted neurotransmitters which blocks the synapse from sending the desired information. The negative emotion fills that neuro gap and takes up residence there.

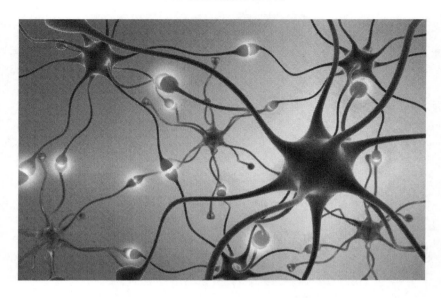

For example, I worked with a woman who felt she was ugly, even though people were constantly telling her how beautiful she was. Something happened in her past that left the impression in her neurotransmitter that she was ugly. Maybe someone told her she was ugly, and, for whatever reason, she believed it, which triggered a series of emotions in her. That thought came in through the neuron and as it was leaving and going through the synapse, her emotions caused the thought to leave an impression. From then on, it didn't matter how many times someone told her she was beautiful because when the *You're beautiful* signal would in, the signal was changed as soon as it jumped that blocked neuro gap. *You're beautiful* became *No, you're ugly.* Even though logically she may think, "They keep telling me I'm pretty and I'm beautiful, so I must be," emotionally, it doesn't feel that way. There's a disconnect between emotion and logic. There's a battle going on, and it's all going on in that synaptic gap.

The key is to diffuse that emotion by unblocking that gap, and then refilling it with what you want to be true. When you do that, there is no reason on this planet that you can't achieve and have anything you want. If I'm shooting for a goal and I'm not there yet, I know it's because I have some screwed-up signals, and I need to reprogram my brain.

I hope you're starting to see how powerful this is. When you can understand the process of your brain and how we interpret signals, you can control the results you get in your life. You don't have to be a victim of circumstance. You get to be a creator and create the life you want.

I fought the wrong battle for years. It didn't matter how many times my parents told me they loved me and it wasn't my fault they divorced. Logically there was a disconnect. As soon as they spoke it, it triggered the old message I had engrained in my synapses, *I'm not good enough, and I can't do anything good.* No matter what. Finally, someone who had the necessary skills cared about me enough to help me see what I couldn't see at the time. I learned the real battle was in my heart and in my mind. When I learned that I could diffuse those thoughts and emotions, my life completely changed. I started to connect logic and my emotions and finally feel and believe that my parents really did love me, and that the divorce wasn't my fault. You will find that as you neutralize the negative feelings and messages, you now have the ability to plant positive ones in their place.

As you move forward, you will see that everything I teach is easy to apply and use. However, if it's easy to use, it's also easy not to use. Don't make the mistake of overlooking these tools because they sound too easy, or because they are foreign to you, or because they sound too good to be true. Decide today that you're going to apply these teachings, and you're going to do it now. I know you will, because that's why you're reading this book—you're ready to break free into a new level of living.

CHAPTER FOUR
Emotional Freedom Technique: Bio Tapping

Do you have a goal you are focused on but are not achieving? Do you ever do something that you regret emotionally? If you know the concept of tapping and continue to have these symptoms, then you are not using the technique effectively. Of all the tools I use, the one I'm about to give you is one of the most simple and powerful, if applied correctly. It helps to clear the clouds of doubts, limiting beliefs, and fears that keep you from fully living out your purpose, your passion, and your why. This technique is called many things. (I've heard it called about fifty different names.) It's most popular name is the Emotional Freedom Technique (EFT), so called by its founder Gary Craig. I learned it from Dr. Anthony James, who called it Bio Tapping and taught it to me in conjunction with multiple other therapies from Thailand as I was studying Soma Veda Integrated Medicine. It's the key that unlocked most of the doors to my success, creating the highest net positive value in my energy investment. Metaphorically, we're changing your flat tires and pulling out weeds. Literally, we're changing your neurotransmitters' responses so that you can entirely become the person you were designed to be.

Even if you've learned this technique, I'm going to teach you some things that you haven't heard before. If you think you've already tried this, but you still have negative emotions coming up that keep you from success, you haven't applied it specifically to those emotions. I encourage you to keep an open mind and ask, "How can I apply this with more depth for greater success?" If you have learned to use positive phrases through this process, then this may be a trigger for you. I'm using it exclusively as a release technique, so we are going to use it to identify your flat tires and tap on the negatives. Remember, the point of this process is to get specific on your limiting beliefs and feelings and bring them to your awareness so they can be shifted.

The Process

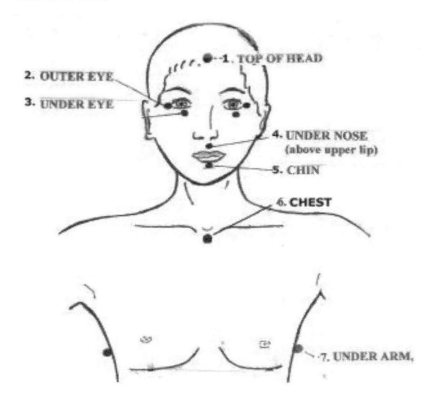

We are going to be tapping on the points labeled in the corresponding diagram. Each point correlates with a meridian line and acupressure point in your body. You will begin at one of two starting points—either the karate chop point, or the chest. I like to start with the karate chop point, which is on the side of your hand, below the pinky where it's soft and fleshy. Some people call the starting point the emotional reversal point, which is the point that helps us reconnect the logic to the emotion.

After tapping the starting point, as explained below, you're going to go through the corresponding points in order on either side, as labeled in the diagram. It's easy to remember the order of points if you remember that they almost exactly follow the shape of a question mark. You start at the starting point (the karate chop point), then move to the top of the forehead, to the outside of the eye, to the point under the eye, then under the nose, then to your chin, then to the chest on the collarbone, where you will use all five fingers, and then finally to your last point just under the arm pit—as shown. As you go through the points, it doesn't matter on which side you do them. You can freely switch sides. Either way, you should feel an immediate shift. It's a very forgiving process; it doesn't have to be perfect. You can totally screw it up and still get great results.

Now let's begin. I want you to actually follow the process and do it in real time as we move through these steps. You're going to be a different person by the time you finish this chapter.

Pick a Negative Thought

The first step in this process is to pick a negative thought, or flat tire, that you'd like to release. Make your selection without judgment. Whatever your emotion is, it's OK. We all have flat tires, and we all have weeds in our gardens. The more vulnerable and honest you are with yourself, the easier it will be for your clients to be vulnerable and honest with you.

Rate the Negative Thought

Once you identify the negative emotion you want to release, rate how strong it is on a scale of zero to ten, with ten being the strongest. This is extremely important. If you're not rating it, it's hard to feel or see results. This will give you a point of reference so that you can measure your success.

Start Tapping

Now, start tapping, using the tips of your fingers, on your starting point. You will tap six to eight times, although that's a ballpark number. It doesn't have to be exact. You can tap four times or you can tap twelve—it doesn't really matter. All that matters is whether or not you get the results. Do what needs to be done to get them.

As you tap, you are going to say what's called your starter phrase. This phrase will embody the negative that you're going to release, following this pattern:

"Even though I_____, I deeply love, forgive, and accept myself."

You will fill in the blank with phrases like:

- wasn't able to accomplish_____because_____
- feel frustrated about_____because_____
- am overwhelmed about_____because_____
- feel like I have too much to do because_____
- don't think I can do_____because_____

Here are some examples:

- Even though I wasn't able to accomplish getting my website done because I don't manage my time well and now I can't launch my business without failing, I deeply love, forgive, and accept myself.
- Even though I feel frustrated about my client not getting back to me fast enough because he doesn't care

about my feelings and now I won't meet my financial goals this month, I deeply love, forgive, and accept myself.

- Even though I feel overwhelmed by learning new things because I still haven't implemented the other lessons I've learned so I'm just adding more to-dos to my ever-growing list, I deeply love, forgive, and accept myself.

The script doesn't have to be exact. However, you'll find that the more specific and narrow you make your phrases, the faster and more dramatically you'll change the neurotransmitters in your brain. The important thing is that you use words and phrases that embody the negative thing you want to release. Most of these may sound logically ridiculous, but it's imperative that you give voice to them. They should trigger the feeling inside of you. If you start talking and nothing is happening, keep talking, using different words and articulating the feeling more specifically, until you are able to resonate with that emotion. Keep tapping on the starting point as you say the phrase. You will say it a few times, still tapping, before you move on to step three.

Tap the Reminder Phrase

Now, you'll move to the next spot at the top of the forehead, and tap six to eight times while you repeat what's called a reminder phrase. The reminder phrase is a short phrase that captures the most painful part of the starter phrase. For example, if your starter phrase is, "Even though I am afraid to talk to prospective clients because I don't feel like I'm valuable enough for them to listen to, I deeply love, forgive, and accept myself"—the reminder phrase might be, "I'm not valuable," or "I always fail," or "no one listens to me." You will repeat a reminder phrase as each point, changing points with each phrase.

You begin at your starting point, tapping and saying your starter phrase, and then move to the point at the top of your forehead (the top of the question mark) and say, "I'm not valuable." Then move to the point on the outside of your eye, "I'm not valuable;" then under your eye, "I'm not valuable;" under your nose, "I'm not valuable;" on your chin, "I'm not valuable;" on the chest, using all five finger tips, "I'm not valuable;" and finish under the arm, "I'm not valuable."

Again, the script doesn't have to be exact. You can change up the reminder phrase from point to point in order to go a little deeper into that emotion. As you're tapping, you may feel certain phrases come to you intuitively; speak those.

Re-Rate the Emotion

Now re-rate the strength of your emotion on a scale of zero to ten. Do you have lingering feelings? If so, this doesn't mean the process didn't work. It simply means that there are still more specific points of that thought, emotion, or fear that need to be addressed. Ask yourself why else you might be afraid, and then articulate your response. The clearer you are, the faster your number will go down.

Often, the fears we have are like branches on a tree. For instance, going back to the example, "I am afraid to talk to prospective clients because I don't feel I'm valuable enough for them to listen to," this fear may stem from a fear of not being good enough, which may stem from an experience you had as a child. If you can get straight to *that* experience and articulate whatever it was that caused the ripple effect in the first place, you'll see the branch-fears diffuse as you diffuse that one. **The key to all releasing is specificity, acceptance, and understanding. So, if you are not getting results, it is because you missed one of these three things.**

If you have lingering emotions, recast your starting phrase and repeat the process, then rate the feeling again on a scale of zero to ten. For instance, if you're working through a feeling of being too busy, you might have started with the phrase, "Even though I feel too busy to do everything that needs to be done in order to organize my business, I fully love, forgive, and accept myself." Then, when you re-rated your feeling, it was still a seven. So, then you would recast your phrase to be more specific, maybe listing all the things you feel are keeping you too busy. "Even though I don't have time to organize my business because I am spending my time taking my children to soccer practice and cooking them meals from scratch and I can't juggle both being a mom and being successful in my business so I'm going to have to give up my dream until my children have all graduated and moved out, I fully love, forgive, and accept myself and my children."

Continue to go deeper into the cause of your negative thought, belief, or emotion until the number is all the way down to one.

Note: You will likely have physical reactions to this process as you start shifting. Whatever your release looks like, let it happen. You may start crying, you may get sweaty, or you may even start laughing or yawning. When I was first learning this technique, I was in a Thai Yoga class. The room was very quiet, and it felt like a sacred time as people were moving through such big feelings. Then I just burst out laughing. Everyone looked at me. I couldn't stop laughing for twenty minutes! I laughed so hard I thought my intestines were going to explode. I had to leave the room and get myself together, but I burst out laughing again as soon as I came back in. Whatever your release looks like, just go with it. If you have trouble with this, seek some help from someone who is getting results. It is all about getting specific, and if you are new to this, it may be difficult to see results until you get the hang of it. This is why it's so important to be sure to rate the emotion you are releasing on a scale of zero to ten so that you can measure your progress. Otherwise, you won't have a point of reference for determining how effectively you are releasing or if there are lingering emotions that still need to be tapped out.

The Shotgun Approach

You can clear multiple negative thoughts in one round. This is called a shotgun session. This is valuable because the faster you can identify and release your negative thoughts, the faster you'll increase your energy input and increase your results. There are a few different ways to do this.

Method One

For the first method, start by going through a writing process. First, identify what negative emotion or behavior you want to work on. For example, maybe it's anger. Once you have identified the issue you want to work on, write down this phrase: "I have this anger because…," or "I get angry because…" Then begin writing whatever comes to your mind. The key here is to keep writing until you have thoroughly explored the feeling. Once you come up with a paragraph, begin another with the same starter sentence, and write down different reasons.

Allow yourself to go deeper and into places that may seem unrelated. For example, you may write after the fourth paragraph about being angry because your dad never let you play soccer when you were eight years old or that you felt like you were invalidated as a child. Whatever comes up, just trust the process and keep writing. After 10 to 20, you should have about five to six paragraphs and be coming to a close. This process helps you get to the root of what is going on and may even need to be done multiple times.

Once the writing is done, begin at the karate chop point and start tapping on the first phrase, "Even though I am angry because…I deeply and completely love and accept myself," then only tap three main points while reading each sentence as your reminder phrase: the forehead, under the eye, and the chest.

For example, let's say you wrote *I am angry because I don't even know why I am angry. I always feel angry, nothing helps me get better. Jim didn't take out the trash and I feel like he doesn't care or listen to me. I am angry because I just don't feel like I know what I am doing and I feel overwhelmed with everything. I just want to give up.*

You would start at the karate chop point and say the first few lines of what you wrote, "Even though I am angry because I don't even know why I am angry, I always feel angry, and nothing helps me get better, I deeply love and accept myself."

Then continue by tapping on the three main points saying the next lines, one line per point. On the forehead, you would say, "I am angry because Jim didn't take out the trash." Under the eye, you would say, "I am angry because I don't know what I am doing." Then you would finish on the chest and say, "I am overwhelmed with everything." While still tapping on the chest, finish with the phrase, "I completely love, accept and forgive myself and Jim (or anyone involved)."

Start again on the starting point and repeat this process until you've read through all of the paragraphs. Be sure and drink a lot of water and take a break if needed. Also, if you didn't get specific enough with some of the phrases, jot done a note or two if you feel like there is something more there that needs to be cleared.

You'll end up spending about ten seconds on each emotion you are releasing. This approach will clear about 80 to 90 percent of your list. Remember, there is an actual biological process your body is going through, so set a pace that won't be too physically overwhelming. Don't be surprised if you feel a little drained afterward.

Method Two

The second method for a shotgun session I want you to practice doesn't require you to do any writing. Below is a list of some common negative thoughts I am constantly finding in my clients. It's likely that many of these apply to you, too, so I want you to tap through this entire list the way you did in the first method I shared. Instead of saying what you've written down, you'll simply be reading from the lists I've shared below.

If you start to feel drained and need to break it up into a couple of sessions, do that, but commit to come back and finish this list. Even if you don't think something applies to you, do it anyway. It may apply even if you aren't aware of it, and it can't hurt you. It can only help. You'll get the shared benefits of going through this list.

- I'm not worthy to succeed.
- I have to struggle to make it.
- I hate money, and I have to work for money.
- I can't be happy unless I have a lot of money.
- It's too hard and complicated to work for myself.
- I'm not good enough to share my message.
- I'll die if I get rejected.
- It's too complicated to talk to people and share my message.
- There's no one around me who wants or needs my message.
- I'm scared to succeed.
- I'm running out of money, which means I'm going to starve.
- The IRS is going to come after me.
- I have to solve their problem now because they're suffering, and it's all my fault if I don't help them.
- I'll just end up losing it all anyway.

- I need a college degree to be able to sell my message.
- I need a website up and cards first for it to work.
- People will think I'm not professional and won't buy from me.
- I can't focus enough to inspire someone to buy my message.
- It's wrong for me to raise my price.

- I'll be taking advantage of others if I raise my price.
- I have to give more than I receive.
- I have to save everyone who doesn't have money.
- It's up to me and my responsibility to help those who can't afford it.
- It's not my fault that I can't afford it.
- It's better to give people a fish, then teach them how to fish.

Now I want you to set a timer for three minutes and make your own list. Write down all your "stoppers." What negatives do you think are stopping you? The more real and honest you can get, the more valuable this exercise will be to you. The more truth you can unlock, the better. Get right into the heart of all the dirty little things that are stopping you. You can do this technique with anything. Try it with allergies, perfectionism, or fears of public speaking, rejection, selling, you name it. If you can think it, you may have already thought it into being, so it's applicable.

I've used this technique personally to transform my life, and I've coached others through this technique to help change theirs. It works, regardless of whether someone believes it or not. In fact, if you're still skeptical, you can even make that one of the negative emotions to clear: "Even though I think the EFT is stupid and it won't work, I deeply love, accept and forgive myself." What you're doing is unlocking these negative thoughts and releasing them so that there is room to add and receive love, forgiveness and acceptance. The longer your list, and the more you clear out, the more benefits you will receive.

If there are some fears you're hesitant to release because you feel they serve you in some way—for example, maybe you have a crippling fear of snakes, as I used to—just know this technique doesn't replace common sense; it's an asset to it. If you remove your fear, it doesn't mean you're going to go pet a cobra. This is just a tool to remove that extra blow, that unnecessary fear that is crippling you.

Once you've made your list, and if you feel physically up to it, I encourage you to do another shotgun session right now to start clearing out some of those fears. You're not going to get through everything today. This will be an ongoing process and an ongoing practice. Go out, share your message, see what comes up, tap it out, then go back out there.

Practice

When I started out, I knew I needed a breakthrough to be successful. I very intentionally went out and did what scared me the most. As I was knocking on those first ten doors, I stopped between each one and took an inventory of what was going on inside of me. I wrote down the answers to these three questions after each door: What did I learn? What do I need to shift? What do I need to change? Then I tapped out the negative thoughts and fears that came up before I drove to the next place, the next door, and did it again.

Knock—rejection.

I went back to my car, answered my questions, tapped out my fears, and then went on to the next door. I did this after every single door and used these rejections as opportunities to learn and grow. I did that all day long. I learned a lot about rejection, about my own value, and that it doesn't matter what others say about my value because it comes from within myself and from my Higher Power. First, I got to where I could talk to people even while I was nervous. As I continued to clear out my emotions, I was eventually able to talk to people without being nervous. As I kept working through my fears, shifts kept happening, and my results kept improving. I challenge you to do the same thing—go out and face your fears as an opportunity to get rid of them. Look at it as practice.

The more you use this technique to release negative thoughts and emotions, the more you become your true self. Each of these negatives are an "other" that you've been carrying around, in addition to the parts that are uniquely you. The more you release, the more room there is for yourself. The more room you have to stand—the more fully you're enrolled in your own life—the more leverage you have to change the lives around you.

If you would like to learn this technique and see it in action, you can check out our *Bridge to Unstoppable* course that goes in depth on some awesome ways to become truly unstoppable. Here is the link: <u>enrollmentmasters.com/bridge</u>.

CHAPTER FIVE
Be Authentic

Now that you've taken the time to start clearing out the garbage, you can get a better view of what's left—you. You have created space for your best parts to flourish. You have unchained your power to create so that you can be the powerful creator of your own life and start making a difference in the lives of those around you. Now that your best self has room to stretch out and take charge, you are ready to master the skills necessary to claim your ideal lifestyle and vision.

You are ready to master the art of authenticity.

Getting to this place of authenticity is essential to enrolling others in your program, product, service, or network. However, even more important, it is central to enrolling them in their own lives—and you into yours. It's the key to success in all things. If you want to have amazing relationships, wealth, happiness, and health—and you want these things to be consistent and constantly in your life—there is no substitute for finding and living from an authentic state of being. I define "authentic" this way: Being true to who you are and being able to truthfully and sincerely express yourself at any time and in any place with anybody. Also, to be in a state of such equanimity that you can receive and communicate with other's beliefs, remarks, and opinions without judgment.

This process is especially important to me because of my own journey to find my authentic and successful self. I spent a large part of my life trying to put on the appearance of success—being in the top of my class in school, a sports hero, a perfect employee—all for the sake of earning back the love I felt I was missing. I spent years living in financial struggle and fear. Subconsciously, I didn't believe that I was worth anyone's investment of any kind. Consciously, I didn't believe I had the resources to invest in anything. However, as I began learning, changing, and applying principles that demand success, I was able to create an amazing business that is impacting hundreds of lives. However, the greatest impact has been on my own life. I am sincerely happy. I no longer wear a mask of success and self-value. My outward success is a reflection of the success and value I have inside.

The Turning Point

What was the turning point? Yes, I learned a series of unique skills and strategies that helped me evolve. However, the true turning point in my numbers came when I learned to be authentic to who I really am. All of the skills and strategies I collected before that were like gathering all the raw materials I needed. Mastering the art of authenticity was the equivalent of using those materials to assemble the vehicle that has moved me forward. I now realize that no matter what happens on the outside, your results are always rooted in your ability to recognize how amazing *you* are, and your ability to live from that place. Success is never a product of what is outside of you. It is not a destination outside of yourself. It is a state of being. Once you turn inward to discover that state, everything else falls into place. You don't have to chase success anymore because it is your shadow.

So, what makes someone authentic? There are many ways, but they all trace back to this one word: *become*. Become authentic. Orient yourself to this way of life. It is the sum of decision after decision after decision of everyday, simple choices that you make. How you treat your clients, how you talk with your family, your relationship with your Higher Power—these are all reflections of your state of authenticity. Do you understand what I'm saying? Becoming authentic means you no longer compartmentalize your life into family, business, faith, and interpersonal relationships. It means you are you, and everything else is a true reflection of who you are. Imagine how much easier it will be to live one life instead of many.

Who Are You?

Tapping into your authenticity is about fully recognizing and manifesting who you are, what drives you, and why you are on this planet. If you don't know who you are, it's going to come across in the conversation when you're trying to create a business or build trust with others in any capacity of your life. It's not going to work. In the movie, *Alice in Wonderland*, Alice drops down the rabbit hole and then all these strange things start happening to her. She grows, and she shrinks, and she has no idea what's going on. When the caterpillar asks Alice who she is, she says, "I hardly know, sir. I've changed so many times since this morning, you see."

"I do not see," says the caterpillar. "Explain yourself."

"I'm afraid I can't explain myself, sir, because I'm not myself, you know."

"I do not know."

"Well, I can't put it any more clearly, for it isn't clear to me."

This is how it is in your life sometimes. You can have great successes, and then things happen, and you shrink down to nothing until you think, "Who am I? What am I doing?" Then you continue on your journey, much as Alice does. As she walks, she comes to a place where the road branches off into many directions with different signs for each possibility. She's trying to make sense of it all when the Cheshire cat appears. She asks the cat which way she should go. The cat says, "That depends on where you want to get to."

"Oh, it really doesn't matter," she says.

"Then, it really doesn't matter which way you go."

Similarly, before we can get anywhere, we have to know who we are. If Alice knew who she was, she'd know exactly where she wanted to go. *You* have a mission and a purpose to your life. In order to identify which roads are going to take you to the fulfillment of that purpose, you first have to answer the question, *Who am I?*

Today, I know who I am, and I'm unravelling my story every day. I am Tyler Watson. I am first and foremost a child of God. I am a loving father and a passionate husband. I help people change their lives and find value inside themselves. I stand for truth, justice, and change. I am a powerful being of light and energy, and I help others see that truth inside of themselves so they can recognize their true potential. I love serving people. I love helping people create money. I love helping people create the lifestyle they want.

The more I find out about who I am, the more I am able to express that to others. I use the tools I have taught you, and will teach you, to keep carving away the "other" parts of me that aren't me. In this way, I can address people as myself—a clear expression of all I want to share and to give to others. Your clients, especially your high-end clients, require this in order to be fully enrolled with you. You must understand in the depths of your soul that there is no competition against you because you are the only you! There's no need to compare yourself to others. Know that even if you teach something like someone else or have the same product, your life story makes you different from all the rest.

The biggest mistake you can make is to wait to share your message because you are trying to find out who you are. You already know who you are! Your history defines who you have become, and the choices of today transform you into who you will be. Bob Proctor puts it best when he said, "The only competition is with your own ignorance." Once you know who you are, your clients can identify where you are taking them, too. It's much easier for them to put your gift on the map of their lives when you give them—when you *are*—clear and precise coordinates.

Your Purpose

Getting to the root of who you are enables you to articulate your purpose and your *why*. When you have a clear purpose and why, you will be pulled toward your goals, instead of always having to push yourself toward them. Changing your habits, releasing your limiting beliefs, reframing your emotional response to negative events—all of these things can sound a lot like walking uphill. However, if you are clear on where you're going and why, you're too busy looking ahead to care about what you have to climb over to get there. You'll see that I am constantly asking you to hone in on your purpose and recalibrate your mindset so that it's centered on that.

Entrepreneurs often lose sight of their why. It gets lost in all the details—the money, the sales, and the numbers. They get distracted by other good or important pursuits and forget the most important one. Do you feel as if you've been there? Perhaps you know where you want to be in business so that you can create a more vibrant lifestyle for yourself and your family, but you find yourself constantly getting so lost in the weeds of making the business work that it's sucking that very vibrancy out of your life right now. It's easy to lose focus. I know I've been there. It's important to hone in on what your purpose is, and then very intentionally keep your focus trained on that purpose.

What *is* your purpose? Why are you doing what you're doing? What is the whole point of putting forth effort, money, time, and resources to grow? It is *not* just to sell, make money, meet like-minded people, or to succeed. Those are all surface reasons. They are the equivalent to planting a seed on top of the ground; they have no depth. If you're just moving forward for these reasons, then you're missing the whole point and you will always be pushing instead of being pulled. The growth you want requires that you have the kind of purpose that will drive you, no matter what is happening outside of you. That requires massive roots.

If your purpose is something like, *I want to make a bigger impact*, that's good, but you need to go deeper. You need to articulate your purpose exactly. This may have many facets to it. For me, the bottom line of everything is to be able to tune in and listen to God. That's my purpose. I want to be able to say, "OK if this is what You want me to do or to be, I'm going to do it and I'm going to become it. If you want me to go in this direction, I'm going to test it. I'm going to go through all the tests, and I want to be able to pass those tests." That's the foundation of my purpose. From there, it branches out into other purposes, building an even stronger foundation for everything I do. For instance, another driver in my life is that I want to provide for my family. I want to create a lifestyle for my family that allows us to accomplish the things that we're supposed to, including serve others and use our gifts to heal and strengthen people. So, what is your purpose? And what *else* is your purpose? Go deeper into this.

Whatever you're doing right now—whatever gift you have—you must always remember that it is a vehicle. It's going to take you to a very specific destination. That destination is going to be defined by what drives you. You're going to make money, and the value of that money is going to be determined by what drives you. You're going to make an impact, and that impact will be defined by what drives you. Even if you don't feel driven right now, you are moving. So, what is pushing you? The point is that whether or not you decide on your purpose, or whether or not you take the time to discover your true purpose and your why, you are going to arrive somewhere. It's going to be better for you and the people you are meant to serve for you to intentionally set that destination.

Some people prefer not to set their destination because they are afraid. They are afraid they aren't good enough to fulfill their purpose. They are afraid that money will ruin them. They are afraid they will fail. They are afraid they will be let down or get hurt. They are afraid of any number of fears that plague us—again, fears that are private but never original. Do not fear your purpose; do not fear your mission. Which is the bigger fear—coming to your death day knowing that you lived a mediocre life and dying with your mission and song still inside you, or all the fears stated above? For me, it is the fear of not sharing my message. Stand for it and be someone who declares it. Be someone who helps others see it in themselves. Be someone who lives your life by faith instead of fear. If you are feeling uncertain, afraid, or crippled, tap it out and keep going. Declare who you are. Speaking your truth is a very powerful way to raise your energy immediately.

What Do You Want?

Make sure you have something to write on because you're going to need it. I'm going to walk you through an exercise that will help you identify the purpose that is going to pull you, instead of the ones you've been using to push yourself. This exercise will give you the right mindset and a runner's high. If you do this every day, you'll constantly be raising that threshold on your life and increasing your results. You will become someone capable of impacting hundreds of thousands of people. No matter how many times you've done this before, you're going to do it again.

You're going to create the vision of what you want.

What do you want? I'm going to ask you five times. Things are going to come to your mind, and I want you to write those things down. Take a minute to get grounded before you begin. Take some deep breaths in, and let them out. In your meditative state, something new will intuitively come to you each time I ask. As you answer intuitively from the creator part of you, some of the answers will surprise you. You may feel you have no idea how to manifest or accomplish the things on your list. Or, you may see how you're already creating them. Regardless of what happens, be open minded and write down whatever comes to you. Don't allow fear to censor your answers. It's important to tap into your intuition here because in order to get to a new level, you need to tap into a higher level.

What do you want?

What do you want?

What do you want?

What do you want?

What do you want?

The answers you've written down are the framework for your ideal lifestyle. Now, your challenge is to create your ideal lifestyle. This creation process starts in your brain. Think it into creation. Write it into creation. Draw it into creation. Do this right now. Hone in on the five things you wrote down, and then use them as the foundation for creating your ideal lifestyle in every aspect of your life. Go to town with your imagination; don't let your logic or your fear get in the way.

What is your ideal lifestyle? What people would surround you? What would you be doing? How many days would you be working each week? How many vacations would you take with your family? How would you be feeling? What kind of house would you live in? What kinds of things would you do in your spare time? These are all part of the details of your building plans. Visualize this lifestyle every morning and night with as much sensory detail as you can. Engage as many of your senses as you can, and always frame your vision in the present tense. This programs your mind to be driven toward it. It will be as if it's already happened.

Get Rid of Dissonance

Create your ideal lifestyle, then begin to mold your life around it—**not the other way around**. If you do it the other way around and build your ideal lifestyle around your current life, you will never achieve it. Period. They don't exist on the same plane. Your life, as is, is not on the trajectory that your ideal lifestyle requires—otherwise, you'd already be living it. You aren't. You have to scrap the framework of the life you've been living and plant your vision, your purpose, your why, and your passion in the middle of your personal universe. These have real power, and you will immediately find that they are the foundation you need in order to build everything else you want.

Right now, take an inventory of the parts of your life you need to scrap because there is no longer room for them in your ideal lifestyle. What are the things in your life that aren't working? What are the rituals, beliefs, or people sabotaging you and keeping you from being your authentic self? These are the things that are creating dissonance in your life. Maybe you're watching too much TV or YouTube, spending too much time on Facebook, listening to too much radio, or just surrounding yourself with too much distraction. Maybe you invest time into good pursuits, but they are pulling you away from your true mission. Perhaps the people in your life aren't very success-minded, or they are pulling you in a different direction than the one you ultimately want to go. Think about the areas in which your life can improve.

Now, choose one of these items you're going to scrap. Pick something you feel is distracting you from your higher purpose. Write it down, then write down what you're going to replace it with. Maybe you're going to read a book, hire a mentor, or meditate instead. Now, honor your commitment to be a 100 percenter and make it happen. Do it. I promise you that as you do this one little thing, your results will start to go up because you're filling your life with good, valuable frequencies. You are what you eat, and you are what you listen to, watch, believe, spend your time on, and think about. Continue to repeat this process of change until you have crafted your entire life around your ideal lifestyle.

Be Your Own Billboard

All of this—your why, your message, who you are, your purpose—brings us back to the importance of being authentic. These individual parts are the layers that make up who you are at your core. As you distill those components of your life, you are prepared to live authentically because you *know* who you are. As you arrive in your own life, you can finally create the reality you've always wanted. If you've struggled enrolling others in the past, it's because you haven't been fully enrolled in your own life. Being authentic—not acting authentic; that's an oxymoron—allows you to be your own walking billboard. Then, you can make more money in a month than you ever have, while offering your unique gifts and living your passions. After a while, it will be as easy as breathing.

I'm going to walk you through a step-by-step process that will give you more clarity in all of these areas so you can live from this place of authenticity. I encourage you to share it with your clients, too. This Authentic Discovery Process, in addition to world-class coaching, is what helped me go from zero to six figures in seven months, while still having the time and freedom to form lasting memories with my family. I want you to experience the same exponential growth. Time, money, love, freedom, and amazing relationships: these are all doors that open with the same key—authenticity.

The Authentic Discovery Process

The following twenty-five questions will help you dig deeply into what sets you apart from other people. This is going to be the core of the message you share with others. Remember, you are your own billboard. *You* are what makes your message totally, powerfully unique. This process is also essential to revealing your why—the core reason you do what you do. Defining your why is as much a process discovery as it is making decision. You will begin to see patterns as you answer the following questions. These patterns are clues to identifying what motivates you to do what you do.

As you go through this process, be present. Eliminate all distractions and take a minute to ground yourself. What you get from this process will be in direct proportion to what you put into it. Answer each question carefully, and look for correlations and patterns. Continue to write until you *feel* finished. Ask your Higher Power to help you come up with answers if you get stuck on something. Afterward, discuss what you have discovered with a partner, coach, or even send me an email. You'll find that the post-discussion will reveal additional layers to who you are.

Note: Being authentic is about being the real you. If I give you a tool or a script that doesn't quite resonate with you, adjust it so that it's something that's coming from your core and captures who *you* are.

1. Who are you? Write down ten different words that describe who you are.

65

2. Why are you on this planet? Write down ten different reasons.

3. What does success look like for you?

4. Why do you want to succeed?

5. What are you most passionate about? What would you do for free if you could?

6. What five things make you unique from all other people you know?

7. What are your three most important successes you have had in life?

8. If you had ten million dollars to create your dream business, what would you create?

9. What would you create if you had $100 million to create your dream business?

10. Because of your dream business, at the end of the day you feel...

11. Your business has made a positive contribution in the world in many ways, such as...

12. Because of your success, specifically, how do you spend your time at home with family?

13. Why do your top three clients buy from you?

14. How much of your success depends on yourself? Others around you? Your circumstances?

15. What does your success have to do with your Higher Power?

16. What kind of energy and effort is it going to take to get where you want to go?

17. What type of relationships do you need to form in order to achieve your goals?

18. What five relationships in your life are limiting your success?

19. What three emotions do you feel slow your success?

20. What are three things that could keep you from being your best self?

21. What do the five most important people in your life say about you?

22. a) What are the top three personal stories that define your life?

    b) How can you use these as a way to teach or inspire others?

23. What are ten new ways that you could create money?

24. When you die, what do you want to be remembered for? What will people say about you?

25. Finish the following statement: "I help people do _____ so that they can have/become_____." (This is going to be what's called your Precision Statement. We'll refine this more later.)

Please don't continue forward until you've taken the time to go through this process. Being authentic is at the core of everything we're going to do from here forward. The last question in particular is something we're going to build on in the next chapter as we discuss how to master the conversation.

CHAPTER SIX
Master the Conversation

As you live from a place of authenticity, The Enrollment Effect ripples beyond your own life to the lives of those around you. The whole purpose of sharing your message becomes to help others enroll more fully in their lives and commit to the changes that will bring them greater joy, success, and fulfillment. How do you do this? Being authentic will attract more and more people to you, but then what? How do you transition them from seeing a light in you to investing in that light? It all comes down to the art of mastering the conversation.

Understanding and Commitment

Mastering the conversation will allow you to intimately understand your clients and lead them to a commitment to change. Every conversation always comes back to those two purposes. This is important, even if I'm not in a business setting and I'm just talking to people I have a personal relationship with—for example, my wife. In that scenario, I wouldn't be as focused on the commitment piece, but I am still seeking pure understanding. By the time we're done with the conversation, the person I'm talking to feels heard and understood, knows I sincerely care about him or her, and we both leave the conversation uplifted and inspired to do better things in our lives. That's my gauge for whether it was a successful conversation.

If I'm talking to people I know are struggling who I want to mentor, coach, or offer an opportunity to, then my goal is to intimately understand them, and to use that understanding in order to help them commit to make a choice that will change their lives. This is true whether I'm talking to prospective clients or current clients. I'm looking to understand them, then get them to commit to the next thing, the next level, or the next movement. If I know that they're in, and they want what I have, then my goal is to get them to invest into my product or service right then and there. If someone has already invested, and they're in my program or and I'm mentoring them, it's still the same conversation—an enrollment conversation. My goal is still to help them commit to doing the action steps, or committing to doing what they know they need to do. I'm always enrolling, regardless of whom I'm talking to.

In every conversation, the Enrollment Effect is knowing that every word you say and every conversation you have is, in essence, transforming people's lives—first by understanding them, and then by leading them to a greater commitment, or enrollment. As you own and recognize that, you become a walking billboard because no matter where you go, you're always changing people's lives. You never let fear, guilt, or shame stop you because you're so keyed in to who you are and your mission, which is to understand and help people commit so that they can become enrolled in their own lives.

You should *never* have a conversation where it's simply, "Hi, nice to connect, see you later," and then leave with the same energy you started with. In every single conversation in your life, your intention should be that by the time you're done, you're going to get to know that person so well that they feel better about themselves, and you feel better about yourself, and you both leave with greater joy. On top of that, you're going to help them commit to improving something in their lives. In doing that, it's a win-win all the way around.

Now that you know the purpose of the conversation, let's discuss the mechanics of actually mastering the conversation.

The Precision Statement

When you're exploring whether someone is going to be a good client, I call this the pre-strategy session. In order to start that process, you need to be prepared with your precision statement, which is patterned after the last question in your Authentic Discovery Process. Here's the formula for your precision statement: When someone asks you what you do, you respond by saying, "I help people_____ so that they can do/have/become_____."

For instance, when someone asks me what I do, I usually say something like, "I help mentors, networkers, and healers package their gifts and enroll high-paying clients so they can actually go on vacation with their families and have the financial support that they want." Here are some other examples of powerful precision statements (if you see something you like, make it yours):

- "I help individuals overcome and heal from addiction so they can clarify their vision and communicate it clearly to others."
- "I help small businesses turn their dreams into realities so they can impact the world while doing what they love."
- "I help entrepreneurs heal their relationships and master their emotions so they can impact hundreds of thousands of lives, double their value, and live with passion."
- "I help highly committed people clarify their life's purpose and focus their vision so they can double their confidence and live their passion."
- "I help young women discover their divine self-worth so they can achieve their goals ten times faster."
- "I help businesses grow through networking, advertising, and sponsorships so they can double their success and make an impact in the community."

You can see that each of these is really precise and immediately communicates the exact kind of client you're looking for, the problem you're positioned to solve, and the results your clients get by working with you. People are always listening for the results. If you just say, "I help people master themselves," what does that even mean? It's too vague. Instead, say something specific like, "I help people master themselves so they can double their income and have the time and freedom to go on vacations, and have the power and influence to make an impact on the planet." The latter gives them something specific to emotionally latch onto. Their immediate thought might be, *Oh, I want to make a difference on the planet—I want that!* By you being precise, yet thorough, people can quickly recognize how what you do matters and how it's relevant to them.

Take Immediate Action

Write out your precision statement by completing this sentence:

"I help people_____so that they can have/do/become_____."

Don't get caught up in trying to make it perfect. It will take refinement, and the more you share it, the easier it will become to share. I continually change mine. This is just meant to be a simple and effective way to tell people what you do.

The Pre-Strategy Session

So, now you have your precision statement, but then what? How do you actually lead them to the strategy session? I'm going to give you some structure on this, but remember that it isn't the structure that makes this work. It's the authenticity and the organic flow of your own personality that works the real magic.

I'm giving you some structure, but I want you to take these principles and plug in your own voice so that it resonates with you when you're talking to others. You don't want to sound like a robot reciting some sort of script. This should sincerely come from your heart, which will immediately transform any conversation into an effective pre-strategy session.

When I'm at networking events and applying these strategies, 95% of the time, I don't even get asked, "What do you do?" That's because I initiate the conversation and take the lead within the first sentence or two. It's easy to do because I ask powerful, intentional questions, and people love talking about themselves. They never even get the chance to ask me what I do because we immediately jump in to enrolling them in their lives. It's so awesome to watch the transformation because once they do, they're unstoppable. You make that person invincible.

I'm going to walk you through it, step-by-step.

Following the Thread

When I'm starting a conversation with someone at a networking event, I first ask a question, then apply a strategy I call "following the thread." It may go something like this:

"Hey, I'm Tyler. What's your name?"

"Hi. My name is Joe."

Then I repeat back their name. That's very important. Most people have their own agenda when talking to others, especially at a networking event, and they don't repeat back the name, which immediately loses the whole point of the conversation. How can you understand someone when you don't even remember their name? So, I say, "Hi, Joe. What do you do for a living? What brought you to this event?" This is where I'm leading him into a more intimate conversation, but in a natural way. I'm just starting with a casual icebreaker to get him to open up.

He may respond with, "Oh, I'm at this event looking to deepen my inspiration and get more motivated in my life."

Boom—there it is. My opportunity. As soon as he says that, I'm going to follow the thread. This process is key. The steps are to *ask, listen, repeat, and relate.* You do that over and over until you get to the commit. You're going to do it three, six, ten times—whatever it takes to get you to the point where you are able to uncover a need that you can fill, whether it's for themselves or for someone they know. Remember, the point is to intimately understand the people you're talking to. You will do that by asking, listening, repeating, and relating. You ask a question, sincerely listen to the response, repeat back to them what they've said so they feel heard, relate to what they shared by sharing one of your stories or something from your own life, and then follow that up with another question, and so begins the cycle all over again. You're gently digging for some pain points that they want to change, at which point, you will naturally move the conversation to the commitment piece.

I call this process "following the thread" because every person is a tapestry. If you look on one side, it's a beautiful embroidered picture. But if you look at the back, it's just a bunch of gnarly threads that work together to make up that beautiful picture. Every word someone says has meaning behind it. Every word is a thread that helps to make up that person. If you want to honor people and truly understand them, you need to follow their threads, and not force yours on theirs. If you can do that, then they will feel heard and understood, and share things with you they never would have otherwise. This is one of the of the most powerful processes you can ever take someone through.

Let's break it down.

So, I'm talking with Joe, and he tells me he's at the event to deepen his inspiration and find more motivation in his life. Most people at this point would say, "Oh, that's cool," and then they'd continue to steer the conversation back to themselves without even having listened to what Joe just said. However, you're going to respond differently, which is immediately going to make you stand out.

"So, you're looking for more motivation and inspiration? That's awesome." Then I'm going to ask him a question directly related to what he just said. "What are you searching for more motivation to do?" I want to use the words he just said because it will keep him on the thread I've identified I want to follow, and trigger the answers I'm looking for. It's going to bring out something that's really important—the thing he's really looking to change, which is where the commitment piece comes in later. If you don't use his own words here, it's going to change his answer, and probably the entire topic of conversation all together. Here, I've used his own words to frame the question, "What are you searching for more motivation to do?"

Joe says, "Oh, I don't know. I just haven't felt really motivated lately. I'm frustrated with my business, and I just don't know what I'm doing. That's really why I'm here." He's sharing something shallow, but it's clear that this is a thread worth following.

At this point, I've asked a question and listened to his answer, so now I'm going to repeat, and then relate by sharing a vulnerable, personal story. "You're here because you want more motivation because you don't feel like you know what you're doing? Holy cow, I've actually experienced something similar to that. I used to come to these events because I didn't feel motivated in my life either. I was trying to grow my business, but it was really hard because I thought I was doing something that I really enjoyed, but when I didn't see the results, I got really burnt out. There was actually a time in my life where I went to an event and I left feeling so bummed because I didn't know who I was, what I was doing, or how the heck I was going to provide for my family. I almost gave up on myself.

"However," and then you spin the story, "I've learned some powerful things in my life using some powerful processes. I finally found my mission." (Then you want to repeat back to them what he was looking for—but *only if it's true*.) "I finally found the motivation and the inspiration to truly live my passion, and it's been phenomenal."

This brings us to a pivotal moment in the conversation. Often, people will share a vulnerable story as a natural way to build connection. However, that's also where you are most prone to lose the intimacy of the conversation because then there's this awkward pause where you expect the other person to respond and carry on the conversation, but they don't. Most people suck at conversations (it's just the truth of it—I used to be that way), so there may be an awkward silence and then the conversation loses its thread, and you move on to something else or just say, "Nice talking to you, good luck with that. See you later." You miss out on an opportunity to change someone's life.

In order to avoid that, as soon as you're finished sharing your story, you immediately go back to the process: ask, listen, repeat, and relate. You just related by sharing your story, so now you follow that up with another question.

"So, Joe, I really get that you're looking for this motivation and inspiration. If you found this inspiration and motivation, what would you do with it?" Here, I'm starting to ask questions about his vision and what he wants to accomplish. I'm emotionally moving him from his pit, which we'll cover more in the next chapter, and offering him a glance at the possibilities. This will begin to open him up, but it will also reveal what he wants to create or change. It's just a mini version of a strategy session.

I keep him talking—following the thread and continually moving through the process: ask, listen, repeat, and relate—and eventually I get him to a point where he says something like, "Yeah, if I found my motivation, I don't really know what I'd do."

At that point, I may have to relate again to open him up, so I'd say, "I get it. That's why you're here. But let's just imagine stepping into this. That's what I had to do to find my own answers, and it's what I do for a living now; it really does work. So, I'm just curious, on a scale of one to ten, ten being the biggest priority for you to find your motivation and inspiration, and zero being it's not important to you at all—you just sit on the couch and veg out the rest of your life—where would you rate yourself on how badly you'd like to change your current level of motivation?"

"Well, I'm here, so maybe an eight."

"Great, an eight. Cool. So, I'm just curious, in order for you to reach your ultimate motivation, what number do you think it needs to be in order to get what you're looking for?" Here, I'm bringing awareness to him.

"I probably need to be at a ten."

"Yeah, probably." (Be sure to agree.) "So, what do you need to do to be at a ten?"

"I don't know. I just really need to decide that I want it, I guess."

"Cool. So let's say you decide that you want it. If you did have that motivation and inspiration, what would you create?"

Then, he'll start to open up and share his vision, to which I'd respond by relating again, and then we're ready to move into the commitment piece because, at this point, I know that his pain point—that he's looking for motivation and inspiration, but hasn't found it—is something I can help him with. Up to this point, I was helping him get clarity and awareness about his pain so he would be ready to do what it takes to make it go away. Now we're ready to move into the commitment piece, which in this case is going to be an invite to a strategy session.

Here's the verbiage for inviting someone to a strategy session:

"So, Joe, you mentioned that you are at a ten in wanting to find that motivation and inspiration, which is why you're at this event. As you know, I've gone through this myself, and I want to share with you some insights. I actually have a seven-step program called The Impact to Income program. Number one, it helps people find their motivation and inspiration" (bring it back to what they're looking for, *as long as it's the truth*), "so they can then live their passion and go and get their dreams. What are your dreams?"

He may say, "I want a new house. I want to get out of debt." And then I'd repeat those back to him because I know they have meaning to him. I'm not just going to say I help people achieve their dreams—I'm going to be specific to his dreams. I sincerely want to help him feel understood, and I also want to remember what his unique dreams are. When he enrolls in my program, and I'm working with him one-on-one, I need to keep in mind what he's striving for so I can help him get those things.

Then, I'll continue and say, "I offer a strategy session that can help you begin this process of finding your motivation and inspiration. It's normally five hundred dollars, but since I have met you at this event and you're serious about this (you said you're at a ten), I'll tell you what—I'd love to sit down with you and *give* you these seven steps, at no charge, so you can start to apply them right now to increase your motivation and help you get XYZ," (XYZ being the restatement of his specific dreams).

Here, the obvious question on his mind is going to be, *What's the catch?* So, you're going to just go ahead and diffuse that right out of the gate.

"It's free. It's normally five hundred dollars, but I just want to give it to you. I'll sit down with you, and we'll over your goals and your XYZ, and then I'll share some other opportunities that you can get plugged into if they're a fit."

As soon as I say that, he knows that I'll be making an offer—that he's not just coming there for a little chat, but with a specific intention to get some help on his goals and to see if what I have is a fit for him. Here, the next question on his mind is going to be, *I just met you, and if I don't like it, will we still be friends?* So, you pre-emptively address that by saying, "If it's a fit, we'll get you plugged in. If it's not, that's OK, no big deal. If something doesn't resonate with you—although, based on what you just said, I know it's going to resonate with you and you'll want to get plugged in because it's going to change your life—" (you're showing a positive, confident attitude about your program and planting that vision of change), "—but if not, it's OK, no big deal. At least I can still give you those seven steps so that you can begin your journey of finding your motivation and helping you achieve your XYZ."

Right there in that dialogue, I've diffused the fear of getting sold, and the fear of not being able to say no. Then, you want to go through the next piece, which is to double up on the commitment part by saying something like, "Joe, let's meet tomorrow at 7:00...," at which point you go over all the details of your meeting. "Do you want to meet via Skype, or meet in person? I know this is important to you, so what will work best for you?" He'll let you know when and where.

This is a good place to drop in a thirty- to sixty-second version of your core story in order to solidify his emotional commitment to showing up. If it fits, pull in some of the words he said into that story. For example, I might finish off by saying, "Joe, I really appreciate your talking with me. I'm really excited to teach you. I just want to share a story with you about why it matters so much to me. I really got plugged in to being a speaker and a coach because of something that happened to me when I was twelve years old.

"My whole life, I thought family was supposed to be the foundation to everything. But one day, I remember my dad coming to me and saying, 'Tyler, your mom and I are getting a divorce.' In that moment, as the oldest son, I took on the belief that it was all my fault, but I wasn't able to articulate those feelings and they just silently drove me from then on. From that moment forward, my motivation and inspiration were shot. I looked for false motivation. I went out and got straight A's, and I was the MVP, but at the end I felt completely empty and void of purpose and meaning. I always fell short of what I wanted to feel. I fought through depression for eight years with thoughts of suicide rambling through my head—wondering if I was good enough to even exist on this planet. But as I learned these seven steps that I'm going to share with you, it was really life changing. So much so that today I've created an amazing business and been able to help hundreds of people find their motivation and inspiration and to achieve their goals and make their impact. I help people come out of their pain and into their success so they no longer have to hide, but can step into their greatness. That's why I really want to share this with you, Joe, because it *really* does matter. It's been one of the most impactful things of my life."

Sharing your story here solidifies the emotional tie you have with your client because in sharing your core story, you're gathering all of those threads that you've been following and making them into one beautiful picture for him to see. Now, all of his focus and his energy is on wanting to know more and to change *now*. He wants to be with you and to hear you because of all the time you just spent with him. He knows you intimately understand him because you were able to articulate back to him the core of the whole point of everything.

Pre-Strategy Session at a Glance

That's it—the pre-strategy session. Here's a review of the steps you're going to follow:
1. Ask a question to start getting to know them.
2. Share your precision statement.
3. Follow the thread—ask, listen, repeat, relate—to uncover a need you can fill.
4. Commit them to a strategy session.
5. Share your story/testimonial.

Tips to remember:
- As you move into the invite piece, pre-emptively diffuse objections and concerns by mentioning that you're going to share with them some opportunities, and if it's not a fit, OK, no big deal, but at least you want to take them through this process to help them get closer to their dreams.

- Always look for and take advantage of opportunities to tie the conversation back into the threads that they shared with you.
- Be extremely thorough as you set the details for the strategy session: day, time, and where. Make sure you've swapped all the necessary contact information.
- Be sure to end with your excitement and confidence about the next meeting.

That's the process for a one-on-one, but you can do this process through any form of media. It's just easier to practice person to person. Once you've mastered this conversation, though, you can do this from stage, online, in webinars—you can do this anywhere you go. It's just a matter of following peoples' threads and helping them make commitments. It's so much fun to watch people transform through this process.

The entire process can take as little as five to seven minutes. The conversation may be longer at first, but as you get more and more comfortable with the process, you'll be able to quickly move a cold prospect to being a warm lead in just a few minutes. Either way, the end result is the same—you have a prequalified client who is committed to sit down with you to hear what you have to offer. You're halfway there. You already know that they are interested and committed because they rated their desire to change at a ten. If the person you were talking to isn't quite at a ten yet, or isn't a fit for your services for some reason, ask about someone else who might be a ten.

No matter the outcome, there's an opportunity behind every person.

Practice, Practice, Practice

Now comes the part where you have to actually do it. Don't make the mistake of waiting to apply these principles—do it *right now*. Find an event and start practicing immediately. I'm serious. Expect a learning curve. The faster you get out there and start practicing, the sooner you will be able to master the conversation. There was definitely a learning curve for me. However, now it's second nature, and it just flows.

I challenge you to talk to fifteen different people doing this pre-strategy session. Out of those fifteen people, you're guaranteed to get one or two who are going to enroll with you because you've talked to enough people at that point for the numbers to start working for you. Once you do, it's just a matter of duplicating the process. The only way to close the gap between here and there is to start moving, so get up and go.

CHAPTER SEVEN
Build Your Package

Mastering the arts of the conversation and stories is vital but will get you only so far in your enrollment process. Some of the Big Fat Problems you will run into when you begin to share something, no matter how authentic, include feeling unsure of how to create and share something of value, having a hard time taking your client in a clear direction from beginning to end, having an end in mind but being unsure exactly how to get there, or being unable to clearly communicate your message with your potential clients.

Now we're going to focus on solving all of these concerns. The solution is to create a package. This will keep you organized in your presentation, build remarkable value for the client, and create a seamless enrollment process from beginning to end.

When my mentor and good friend, Ted McGrath, first taught me how to package my material, it made a night-and-day difference. Two days after I created my package, I was sitting next to a stranger on a plane. We started talking, and I used all the tools I'm teaching you—I led with my precision statement, and then went through the steps in my package. By the end of our one-hour flight, she'd committed to a strategy session. She enrolled in a $1,500 package. Prior to that, I was trying to share my message with several different companies, but I was struggling to articulate exactly what it is that I do. This affected my self-esteem. My self-confidence plummeted, and when I went to share my message, everything just felt really off. Have you ever shared your message but you could tell the person you were talking to didn't value it like you do?

Ted taught me how to hone in on my message and my gift by creating a package. If you're already working with a product that is packaged, such as network marketing, what I'm sharing will still be applicable to you. You'll be able to refine your package even further. However, if you are like me and you're starting from ground zero, this is going to give you the essential clarity you need to move forward.

How to Build Your Package

Your package is going to follow this format: Problems, Solution, Benefits, Tools and Resources. So, the foundation of your package begins with identifying the problems currently facing your clientele. I'm going to share three different methods for identifying those problems. Pick the one that feels the most authentic to you, and then go with it. Each of these methods, or a mix of all three, are effective for coming up with the core questions that will serve as the base to your package. (It will make more sense as we go along.)

Method One: Define Your Niche

The first method centers on your ideal clients' main problems that you are positioned to solve. So, who are you ideally serving? Imagine you have the whole world in front of you and you are playing that claw arcade game where you move the joystick around to determine where the claw is going to drop. If you have the entire world to choose from, and you could choose any person on the planet—putting all your limiting beliefs aside—who would you want to work with? Make your selection, then drop the claw precisely over that person and let it close around your ideal client. (Don't worry; it's a nice padded claw, so it doesn't hurt anyone.) Then drop that person down into the chute. Who is this person? What's his or her story? Get as clear as possible about who this person is—what he looks like, what she does for a living, his income bracket, what is most important to her, and where he can be found spending his time.

Entrepreneurs often feel as if their ideal client is everyone. If that's your thinking, I invite you to change it. Believing you can help everyone actually translates into helping no one. The more specific you are about who you're looking for and who you can serve, the better referrals you're going to get. If I reach out to my network and say, "Hey, I would love a referral," the automatic response is going to be, "Who are you looking for?" You don't want to say something so vague that no specific person comes to mind. You want to give a response that makes a *name* come to mind. As soon as you get specific, your results will double and triple immediately. You're going to get better referrals for better clients, and you'll be able to bless more people.

Take Immediate Action

For example, here is my story for the people who enroll in my eight-week course:

> Every single person who is plugged in for the next eight weeks is a high achiever and highly motivated to succeed. They unlock the passion deep inside of them so they can go out and share their message with one person, and then the next, and then the next. They make a huge ripple effect that changes lives. As they continue to share, they come to master the enrollment conversation. They begin sharing packages starting off at $1,997, and as they form their beautiful package, they get connected with the very people they know they're supposed to be with. In the conversations, they become excellent listeners. They find and unlock the passion in others. As

---

they get more engaged with others, they find more joy and a deeper purpose and mission in their own lives. They find great joy in all the little things, and they're having fun sharing their message. Their packages allow them to free up more time to do what they love. These people are amazing, and they give me high-quality referrals and testimonials.

Once you've identified your ideal client, write down seven to ten common problems currently facing the specific people you want to help. These problems will be the basis of your system, or your package.

As your clients' peers see them changing, they're going to seek you out for their own transformations. From there, it's a ripple effect across masses of people, all of whom you'll be helping and serving.

Method Two: Based on You

The second method comes in handy if you are new to the game, are still in the process of articulating your message, and you don't have an ideal client yet. In this case, you're just going to use yourself as the sample client and articulate the main seven to ten problems that you personally have faced and overcome. This should be fairly straight forward, but if you get stuck, The Authentic Discovery Process you completed in the last chapter may offer some clues. Here are three additional questions to help get your juices flowing:

1. What is the main problem you have faced and see others similar to you facing?
2. What is a common problem you see in people around you that you wish people could change? For example,

maybe you see that people are slaves to money, or perhaps they aren't managing their businesses well.

3. What are you so passionate about that you're already doing all the time for free?

The best way to articulate your message isn't necessarily to go through a process to figure it out. The best way to get clarity on your message is to just get out there and share the message that you're passionate about, and to enroll clients into that, whatever it is. You will likely attract clients who are representative of you, of your past self, because your passion is likely going to be based on who you are and what you've gone through. You can help anyone, as long as they are at least one step behind where you are right now. If you don't know where else to start, start there. There's no magic formula for doing it; doing it *is* the formula. From there, you will get clearer and clearer on who your ideal client is and the makeup of your specific niche.

Method Three: Reverse Engineer the Solutions

The third method is to reverse engineer what you're currently offering in order to identify the problems it solves. Start by writing down all the tools you use to get results, and then write out seven to ten specific problems that those tools solve.

Creating Your Package

You should now have worked through the method you are going to use and have a list of 7-10 problems facing your specific niche. Each of those problems is going to be a step in your package, and each step will have each of these components:

- Problem
- Solution
- Benefits
- Tools and Resources

Generally speaking, your package is going to have about seven steps, based on the number of acute problems your ideal client is facing and you are aiming to solve. You don't have to have exactly seven. You can have more, and you can have less. However, you definitely need to have more than two. Look back over the actual problems your clients have. Go through and label them in descending order of most common problems. This will help you identify where you need to start, and which progression is going to make the most sense.

Your goal is to ask yourself, "If I want to take a client through a transformation process, what's the first thing I need to help them with?" They have something stopping them. Maybe physically they're in pain or spiritually they're depressed. They've got some sort of issue that's unsolved. Maybe part of the issue is that they feel they've tried everything and spent all their money looking for solutions, but they haven't gotten results. The solution is to break it down and figure out exactly what's stopping them so you can help them change. Be very specific, but also be fluid. I'm always refining and upgrading the details of my package. It's not like "this is the only way it ist." It will always upgrade and change as you upgrade and change.

This is a simple and straightforward process. You just simplify the problems, simplify the benefits, share the tools, and list two to three benefits for each tool. The simpler and clearer it is, the easier it will be for your clients to understand exactly what you're offering and where you're taking them. You can look at my template to get an idea of how to do this.

Take Immediate Action

I want you to start creating your package right now as we go through this process. Select three problems currently facing your ideal client, and do the work as I take you through the process.

Download a blank copy here, and begin filling yours in as we go: https://authenticenrollments.com/blueprint.

Impact to Income System Blueprint

Step	Problem	Description/Solution	Transformational Benefits	Tools and Resources
Step 1: 30 DAY DASH FOR CASH	Taking too long to get clients. Unable to communicate with your network.	Focus and refine for 30 days to get results quick	✓ Begin mastering the enrollment conversation ✓ Create money within 30 days	✓ 30 Day Dash for Cash webinar ✓ Blueprint ✓ Calls and check ups
Step 2: THE PRECISION STATEMENT	Customers get turned off within 1st 6 seconds of a conversation.	Be crystal clear about what you do and how it serves the customer	✓ Complete confidence in networking ✓ People will want what you do within 1-3 min of a conversation	✓ Precision Statement Formula ✓ Clarity Niche Process
Step 3: BUILD YOUR PACKAGE	Customers don't see the value you see.	Present information with expert clarity and inspire others to take action	✓ Get high end customers ✓ Own your product/service ✓ Guide anyone through a transformational proven process	✓ Program Builder ✓ Program Builder Template
Step 4: MASTER YOUR STORY	The customer leaves uninspired to act.	Master your 30sec and 60 sec story in sales	✓ Gain confidence ✓ Form lasting relationships with your clients ✓ Connect in ways that others in your profession won't	✓ The Story Module ✓ Voice Mastery ✓ Create your story
Step 5: HOW TO MAKE AN OFFER	Not able to make a powerful impression, lacks authenticity, uninspiring, closes the client. Client feels "sold to"	Open your client and sell them on themselves diffusing any objection with precision	✓ Freedom from rejection ✓ Confidence in every sale ✓ Make the offer the most exciting part of the whole process	✓ The Journey Sequence ✓ Diffuse Objections
Step 6: BREAK FREE PROCESS	Underlying fears paralyzes the delivery and no techniques to overcome negative emotions	Gain clarity and precision with your emotions and eliminate self-destructive programs	✓ Master your emotions ✓ Have powerful tools to use the rest of your life ✓ Become fearless in delivering your message	✓ BioTapping ✓ Shotgun approach ✓ Expand the bubble
Step 7: DOUBLE YOUR VALUE	Not able to cross the money barrier and clientele are more of a burden than an inspiration	Gain control over money, learn to enjoy the process	✓ Double your worth/or fees ✓ Gain the clientele you are seeking ✓ Earn back more than what you invested	✓ Money Mindset tool ✓ Find Your Worth Process
Step 8: INTEGRATE AND CHANGE	What is taught is forgotten and no preparation occurs before sales	Selling becomes second nature and you play at your best	✓ Selling is an inspirational conversation ✓ Know exactly what to do for your client	✓ Pregame Tools ✓ Daily Routine

The Problem

For each step, you first have to identify the problem that you're solving. What's the point of creating a package if you're not solving a problem? This is the core of the whole process. Skipping this step and going straight into talking about the tools you're offering is a turn off instead of a turn on. People aren't just looking for solutions in their lives. They are looking for *specific* solutions to *specific* problems. Once you can articulate the problem they are facing, you will have their attention as you share the solution, and you'll be able to enroll them into $2,000 to $10,000+ packages. If you can become a master problem solver, you'll have some pretty good job security.

The Solution

The next essential component is the solution. The solutions are what you're offering to people. This blueprint is a very clear and simple way to express that. For example, looking at my template, the first step is The Precision Statement. The problem is, "Customers gets turned off within the first six seconds of the conversation." The solution is, "Be crystal clear about what you do and how it helps the customer." Write down your solutions now for the first problem you are solving.

The Benefits

Here, you're going to highlight the benefits and results you'll get from the specific solution you offer. Highlight both the tangible and intangible benefits. For instance, going back to my example, the benefits to mastering the precision statement are, "Complete confidence in networking," and "People will want what you do within one to three minutes of a conversation."

This part of the process is critical. In the words of Jim Rohn, "When the promise is clear, the price gets easy." When you can give them a clear vision of the benefits and results, people don't care about the price. Now, write down three benefits and results for the first problem you are solving.

Tools

The tool is very important because once you make a promise, people want to know how you're going to make good on that promise. What are you teaching them that unlocks those results? How have you received that result? The kind of tool isn't as important as the fact that it *is* a tool.

The wording is important for the left-brain people, so use words such as processes, tools, questionnaires, books, CDs, modules, formulas, builders, masteries, sequences, approaches, and routines. Thinking in terms of tools is a way to rename what you already have. It's all about effectively communicating what you do. For instance, if you have a great questionnaire in PDF format, don't just say, "I'm sending over a PDF for you to fill out." Instead, say, "I'm sending over the Find Your Niche Process, which is a list of twenty-six different questions that will help you hone in on exactly what your niche is." Then people are going to pay attention. Or, if the problem you're addressing is that someone has tried everything and hasn't been able to get a solution, the tool that you take them through may be a questionnaire or a process that identifies the emotional blockage keeping them stuck. Or maybe you create a formula called, "The 'Uncover The Core' Formula," or "The 'Unravel the Core' Process."

The more tuned in you are to how you can help people, the more thoroughly you can address and solve their problems. People will see that and want what you have to offer. Now, write down the unique tools you have to offer that solve the first problem.

Step Name

Now that you have the entire first problem outlined, give it a powerful name, and write it down in the "step" section. This helps you communicate what you do to your clients. Let's say John Doe needs help making money in the health industry, and you are a network marketer looking for builders. Your first step could be called "Gain the Vision." The entire first-step process would look like this:

- **Step**: Gain the Vision
- **Problem**: Unsure how to make money and be healthy at the same time.
- **Solution**: Use and understand the XYZ product and share with others
- **Benefit:** Live a healthier lifestyle, make money doing what you love, etc.
- **Tools:** XYZ product, jump start kit, enrollment system.

BOOM! You just created your first step, my friend.

Rinse and Repeat

Now you just have to repeat the process for all of your steps. Again, the wording is important, so give each step a title that is both descriptive and powerful. Once you have done this for all of your steps, your package is complete and ready to share. Your steps will be progressive, meaning you will start with step one, go to step two, and then on to step three, etc., but you don't necessarily have to take your clients through the steps in that exact order. If someone needs step four, then start there. Focus on the needs of the individual. For example, my step five is the breakthrough process. If I'm talking to someone who is operating from a place of crippling fear, then I know I need to take him there immediately.

The whole purpose of this format is so you can:

- Share your message with precision.
- Be clear about what you're offering.
- Create an order to your presentation so it's easily understood.

- Easily repurpose your content into classes, workshops, online presentations, one-on-one mentoring packages, and more.

Most important, your package is for you, as it makes it much easier for you to serve your client and fulfill your purpose. You can use this as the template for your one-on-one presentation, a speaking presentation, a webinar series, your sales process, an e-course—the possibilities are endless. It's there to serve you anytime you need to be able to communicate and share your gift in a way that it can be optimally received. This helps you stay organized and speak intimately to your niche. You can lead a horse to water, but you can't make it drink—but you sure can salt its oats! When you're going out and sharing in this way, you're salting the oats and making your prospects very thirsty for what it is that you're doing.

As your program evolves, so should your stories about your clients' successes. The more you do this, the more you will see what needs to be changed or upgraded. If something feels fuzzy, you just need to ask better questions to get more clarity. The more you practice this and share it, the sharper it will become.

A Work in Progress

Everyone in your niche needs your message, so don't let the need to have everything perfect stop you from sharing it. That is selfish. When I first did this, I totally screwed up my package. I accidentally left out an entire step when sharing it. I was selling a seven-step package that had only six steps, and no one even noticed. I promise, you can be imperfect and still succeed. Accept that you're always going to be a work in progress, and then take as many people as possible along with you for the ride.

CHAPTER EIGHT
Master Your Stories

One of the most effective ways to show your mastery of the authentic conversation is to use stories to connect with your clients. Everything in life is based on a story. The most masterful teachers in the history of this planet—Gandhi, Jesus, every teacher who made a mark—was a master storyteller.

The purpose of using stories is to connect with people in a deeper, more spiritual, more powerful way. If you have ever wanted to leave a lasting impression on someone and gain immediate trust, story is the key. Building that connection is a two-way street. You can't bring your client on this journey without going there yourself. You have to be authentic and genuine. You must be vulnerable and honest enough to share the core of who you are. In this chapter, I'm going to teach you the value of using stories. I'm going to show you how to craft them and then how to implement them as powerful tools. Even if this is a tool you're already familiar with, there's always room for improvement.

The Five Steps to a Powerful Story

There are five steps to a powerful story that inspires others:
1. The Set Up: the background and the details.
2. The Pit: the deep, dark nasty thing that happened.
3. The Journey: how you got out of the pit; possibly highlighting the trial and error.

4. The Transformation: your happy ending and lessons learned.

5. How it's relevant: tie it in to today.

For example, here is my core story. Follow along and see if you can identify the different steps:

When I was twelve-years old, something happened to me that changed my life completely and turned my whole world around. It was summer break, and I was taking it easy sitting on the couch watching television. Life was pretty good. I was the oldest of five children, and I felt positive about who I was and what I was doing. Then everything changed. I remember my mom and dad coming into the room and turning off the TV. I feel this vibe, like something is about to happen. My dad sits down, looks me in the eyes, and then says something I will never forget. (1. The Set Up)

He says, "Tyler, your mom and I are getting a divorce." Emotionally, I hear, "It's all your fault; we don't love you anymore." I feel as if someone is pulling a rug out from under me. My whole life flips upside down.

I spend the next several years striving to prove to myself that I can earn back the love I feel I lost when I was twelve. To make things even more complicated, my mom goes through three more divorces, and my dad goes has another one. The same message resonates in my soul: *I will never make it, and it's all my fault.* There are times that my parents tell me, "I love you so much." However, what I feel is, "I'm not good enough, I don't deserve their love, and no one cares about me at all." I go out and try to prove myself because I think I have to earn love. I get straight A's in school, MVP on my sports teams, I graduate second in my class, and am the class president. However, at the end of the day, I feel empty and alone. I hide behind pornography and video games, unable to tell a soul what is really going on because I believe I have to be perfect and I am afraid to let anyone down. One day, I find myself sitting on the edge of my bed, bawling my eyes out, and wondering whether anyone will even notice I am gone if I kill myself. (2. The Pit)

Fast forward a few years. I get cleaned up to go on a two-year mission for my church. I feel as if I've finally found the answer, which is to serve other people. I finally feel whole and able to connect to God at a higher level. Coming back from the mission, though, I fall into the same old habits and again I think, *I can never change* and *I am not good enough*. It effects my business, and I'm barely making enough to pay the bills. I am afraid to succeed. I start seeking to change. I know that I want to succeed in life, so I begin to read and study new ways of thinking. I meet the girl of my dreams, and I begin to dive into personal development and address things I have avoided most of my life. (3. The Journey)

Through this, I am able to take the blame off of myself and start seeing people differently because I see myself differently. I am valuing myself, valuing my family, and valuing my Higher Power like never before. As I start doing this, my results start to change. The Enrollment Effect starts to ripple through my life as I learn the skills and master the emotions needed to grow a profitable business. I am able to scale my business to make up to six figures each month in just seven months. Within a year and a half, I am generating over a quarter million dollars in one weekend, having time and freedom to spend with family and in church service, and I am able to help others generate massive amounts of wealth and freedom themselves. (4. The Transformation)

So today, I share with people how to value themselves so they can get paid what they're worth. I show them how they can feel good inside and stop feeling that they have to prove themselves, because they're already good enough. I show them how to arrive at that place so that they can deliver their message because it's a message the people on this planet need. And so, Mr. Client, I would love to sit down with you and share with you my strategy that will totally change your life as you implement these several steps and processes that will help you to finally break through and know your value so you can go out and share your message with others today. (5. How it's Relevant to Today)

Were you able to identify all of the parts? I threw in some different bits I don't usually use to show that the story can be a little fluid. It's OK if it's not exactly the same from telling to telling. In fact, it's best if you're not trying to follow an exact script because this *isn't* a script. It's a story. It should be an intimate telling every time. If it's going to resonate with your client, it has to resonate with you first. Tap into the emotion and sincerity you're trying to convey.

Your Stories

What is *your* core story? What do you have inside of you that connects with other people? If you feel as if you're still in the middle of your story, pick something from your past you feel has helped you become who you are today. I hired a coach to help me craft mine. If you need some help with this, reach out to my team or join us at our Impact 2 Income live event, where we all practice this together. The first time I learned how to share effective stories, I wondered what my story was. I didn't feel I had a universal story. Then I started going back, and I thought to myself, *Where in my life have I had some big pits? Some pains and hurts?* I found that I had suppressed many of them. At first I thought, *Yeah, my parents divorced, not a big deal.* I wouldn't even delve into it because I was afraid of what I'd find. However, as you can see, unraveling that has been essential to my authenticity, both with myself and with others. If you're not sure what your pits have been, perhaps some of your universal stories will manifest as you relive some of those moments you haven't wanted to dive into yet. You aren't reliving them for the purpose of feeling pain, but for the purpose of inspiring other people.

This is true for all of your stories, not just your core story. There are several types of stories you can use to inspire others to act.

- Money story
- Time story
- Regret story
- Testimonial story
- Other lesson stories

Basically, you should be prepared to share a story for every objection. When someone says, "I don't have the time to do this right now," you can respond with, "I understand how you feel. There was a time in my life when I didn't want to take action because I felt so crippled by the time demands in my life, too." Or if they say they will do it later, share your regret story. Each of your stories will help connect with your clients emotionally and move them to a place of action. The whole point of creating stories is to share them with people and help to remove their blocks. When someone has an objection, that is a block. As soon as you identify what the real block is, respond with, "I understand," and then go into your story.

For example, when a client tells me they aren't ready to enroll because they don't think they can afford to (and this is probably the block you're going to run into the most), I say:

I understand. I used to struggle trying to figure out how to get paid for what I was passionate about. After I got married, I was even more desperate to make it happen so that I could provide for my family. There was a time when I had just over a grand in my bank account, and financially I was at a low. I am struggling, but inside I had this deep passion to get out of this struggle mentality. I wanted to live in abundance so that I could impact others. Then one December, right around Christmas, I find myself at this event that is pitching a program I know would take me to the next level. The program is $5,400, and I have only $1,500 in my bank account. I know I can't do it, but then I tune in to my Higher Power, and He says to me, "Tyler, who are you going to serve? Money? Or Me?"

I freeze up.

There is this course I know I am supposed to take. It is a door my Higher Power has placed in front of me on purpose, but I don't have the money to open it. I am thinking all this, and again this voice says, "Tyler, who are you going to serve? Money? Or Me?" My wheels start turning, and I think, *I want to serve my Higher Power; I want to serve people; I want to serve others.* It hits me. I realize that if I don't invest in myself, if I don't change, I will be serving money—a slave to money and letting money make my choices. That day, I made a decision. I decided, *I'm in!* I made calls to people, I got loans—I did whatever I had to do to make it happen. I found a way as a creator, and created it. Now I'm creating five to six figures every month, living my passion and my mission and helping others do the same. I didn't let money dictate my transformation; I let my Higher Power dictate that.

I realize that you're struggling with money. When would you like to stop struggling with money? How about now?

This is one of the five money stories I share, and you may also find that you have several stories for each category. You can pick and choose which one is most appropriate based on the person you're talking to, or what you intuitively feel led to share. I decide which one to use based on which story is going to make the biggest connection with the person I'm talking to.

What Not to Do

In addition to the general format you want your story to follow, there are also things you *don't* want to do with your story. Here are some examples of what *not* to do:

- Staying in the pit: This means you get to the doom and gloom of your story, and stay there. Example: *I was twelve-years old, and man, my parents divorced, my life sucked and it still does. I'm not enough, my life isn't working, and I hate my parents because it's all their fault. They've destroyed my life.* When someone shares their story like that, they become someone you want to avoid. Where's the transformation? Where's the happy ending? This is never going to inspire anyone, and it's definitely not going to move them to make an investment.

- Only sharing the transformation: This is when you lead with the awesomeness of what you have without taking them through the process to arrive there with you. This is where most network marketers lose it. For example: *I have this product, and it's the best thing I've ever done. You just have to try it so you can transform!* People will just pat you on the back and wish you luck because they won't feel it's relevant to them. If you lead with this kind of excitement, instead of taking them through the pit and then climaxing, you're failing to relate to them where they are right now. Or, if people do buy into it, it's under false pretenses. They may enroll with the expectation of becoming Superman, and when they realize they are also Clark Kent they give up on themselves. You must relate to them in all ways.

- Rambling on and on and on…: This is when you tell your story as a sequence of line items with no purpose, no emotion, and no point. For example: *When I was twelve, my parents divorced, and it was pretty tough for me, but I overcame it, and I got straight A's and stuff in high school, just*

Take Immediate Action

Now practice your core story. Try to share the entire thing in ninety seconds. Deliver it fast. Don't wait until it's perfect. Even if your story isn't complete, go for it; this will help make it complete. The best way to change is to just dive in with both feet first. Share your story in the present tense. Transport the listener into that moment. This alone will help aid in the transformation for the listener.

For more help, check out thefreedomcatalyst.com to get some free online trainings on crafting your story. Sometimes seeing this presented different ways helps lock it in.

---

trying to prove myself. I learned some good lessons out of it, and I love my parents; they're really great, and it's not their fault. It just kind of is what it is. I don't blame my parents, but I really like to talk to people about their value now. This makes you feel like, "Wah, wah, wah.... Please stop talking to me."

The Cost of Not Sharing Your Story

Mastering your story is critical to your success. Not sharing your story will cost you money. I learned this lesson the hard way. This was when I'm finally getting into my groove. I'm excited about sharing and helping people, and I'm finally getting paid what I'm worth. Then I get lazy. I decide my stories aren't necessary, and I'm going to save time by just sharing the logic of how my program works. So, I meet someone for the first time, and they sit down with me in my office. I start sharing about my programs with her. I ask about her life, where she wants to go, what is her dream—but it just feels as if we aren't connecting. We get to the selling part, and I feel completely off. Right then, I realize I had better use my story. So, I just look at her and I say, "You know what, I forgot to share with you one of the most important things." I share my story, and all of a sudden, the energy in the room starts to change and transform. I feel connected to her. We have an amazing experience, and in the end, she invests.

Fast forward two days. I get a referral from this same woman. I hop on the phone, and the woman says, "Tell me about what you do." I dig right into the logic of my programs. The whole conversation feels superficial. I go on for twenty minutes, trying to save myself. However, I can tell I'm losing her. She doesn't think my program sounds that great. Then the thought comes to me, *share your story!* So, I back up and tell her my story. She says to me, "Tyler, I wish you would have shared that in the very beginning. Right now, I'm just not that interested. Thanks for your time, goodbye." I think to myself, *I just missed an opportunity to change someone's life because I didn't share my story*. I avoided the story. I wasn't authentic, which made a bad first impression.

If you do a strategy session or have a sales conversation without sharing your story, you're going to fail to reach everyone you could have. You may still get people involved because you're a good person with a quality message, but if you really want to connect with others in ways that you've never connected with them before, share your core story. Share it as if it's the most important part of your process, because it is. If someone asks, "What do you do?" go straight to your story. This inspires people. Don't fall into the trap of not sharing. If you feel resistance to sharing your story, go do some breakthrough work and recite it over and over again. Don't get to a point where your story isn't special, because it is. Everyone's story is unique and special and different. People need to hear *yours*. Even if it's similar to someone else's, yours is different, and the planet needs to hear your voice.

When Others Judge Your Story

Sometimes I have students who tell me that they feel judged when they tell their stories. If you feel you're being judged by others as you tell your stories, chances are you are struggling with some unresolved self-judgment. The judgment you see in others is most often a reflection of the judgment you still carry. If you are confident about your story, people aren't generally going to judge you for the details. If this is something that you come up against, do some breakthrough work—using guided meditations, tapping, or hiring someone to help you clear your emotional blocks—and then keep telling your stories. This applies to any struggles you come up against in this process. Push through the barriers, and keep practicing like crazy. The faster you can master your stories, the faster you can successfully use them to enroll high-paying clients.

An Invitation to Be Authentic

Sharing your story opens a two-way door of authenticity. If I'm doing a strategy session with someone who doesn't know me, I share my story and open up first. Often, this invites them to also be open and authentic. They feel safe sharing the real problem. If you don't establish that kind of trust and openness, they are likely going to share a surface problem, which is just a wall that goes up to keep you out. So, in order to save time, share your story first and just initiate the openness right away.

As with most of the principles I'm sharing with you, this principle has a universal application well beyond just working with clients. Any time you want to build trust with anyone, share a story. There was a time when I was working with some young people, and they wouldn't open up and share about the things that were stopping them. I shared my story about struggling with pornography when I was their age. I felt so guilty about it because I was supposed to be this perfect kid. In hindsight, I understand what I was really doing, which was seeking outside of myself for false fulfillment. It was a false food. Afterward, I felt ten times worse, which affected how I treated people. Now, one of my main goals in life is to respect and defend women and womanhood. Women are being put down, and many of them aren't valuing themselves. The inside is so much more important, but the media has it backward, portraying the outside as what is so special. I am so grateful for my wife, because she is one of the most beautiful people I could have ever imagined meeting.

I shared with the youth this story of how I struggled, and also how I had a breakthrough. Then I asked again, "Have you ever struggled with anything like that?" All of a sudden, one boy opened up to me about how he was struggling with pornography, how he was struggling trying to keep his mind pure and doing good and serving and loving people. Then each one shared and opened up to me like a book. This created an opportunity for me to serve them more thoroughly because I was aware of what their intimate needs were. The sad part about this is the parents were clueless on how to get to that place with these kids because they didn't understand the enrollment effect.

This is just one example of why it's so important for us to be real and share our stories. As you share your stories, your relationships will change. Your loved ones will change, and everyone will change to make a difference. If you feel your kids aren't open, share a story. If you want a more intimate bond with your partner, share a story. It doesn't have to be a deep dark story or a confession. It just needs to be something that builds a bridge.

The most important thing is to be you. Be authentic. As you can be you, people will feel comfortable sharing the truth. What if everyone in your family could be real and truthful? Would that make a difference in how everyone shared their truths in your house? If you can be real and genuine in your home, it's going to be easier to be open with your clients because you're already practicing being that person in your daily life. If you're open with your clients, will that change your relationship with your clients? And as you help *them* be genuine and authentic and real in their families and in their communities, you're going to make an impact in *their* lives, in *their* state, in *their* community, and on *our* planet. If we could all just learn to be ourselves, the planet would literally transform.

As you are working on mastering this tool, celebrate the small successes and don't get caught up in being perfect. If you fall short, don't get down on yourself. If you share your stories with someone and they don't enroll, celebrate the opportunity to practice. Once you create this mindset that everything is a success, you never lose. This kind of energy will attract the right people to you. If you have the mindset that you don't have to be perfect to succeed, other people who are imperfect, (and that's all of us) will want to work with you. If you're a perfectionist and everything must be in perfect order before people work with you, no one is going to want to work with you. This all comes back to being authentic and real. So, don't be perfect. Just be you.

CHAPTER NINE
The Strategy Session

Everything up to this point has been a series of building blocks and strategies that will prepare you to master the one-on-one enrollment or the strategy session. If you can master the one-on-one enrollment, you can master the enrollment online, on stages, in webinars—on every platform. If you don't have this piece, you won't have authentic conversations that lead to enrolling high-paying clients.

The most important key to your success is going to be this: **Know what you want**. This is true for everything in your life, not just your strategy session. You have to know what you want in exact detail. The more specific you are in that vision, the more success you'll have. For example, I know I want 75 percent of my ideal audience at my events to enroll in what I'm offering. If I stray from being laser focused on what I want—from my vision—then the results drop. If I do a presentation, and my goal is to get those who are ready to sign up on a piece of paper, I won't leave until they do. I know what I want, and I get it.

I used to fear sales because it was an unknown to me. I had no idea how to do it. Now, it has become one of the most beautiful experiences of my life because it's a process of helping people enroll in their lives. As you're helping them and recognizing you can fill a need, you're simply asking for money in exchange, which allows you to help even more people. It's not a gateway to greed; it's a gateway to service. A strategy session is one of the most powerful and transformational conversations you can have with any human being on the planet. I have had many beautiful conversations with people all over the world.

Even if what you're doing isn't a fit, you can still authentically and genuinely serve them. You can either lead them to someone you know who can help them, or you can give them some tools and resources to help them find the right solutions on their own. In this way, every single strategy session is a win, regardless of the sale, because you are more fully enrolling each person in his or her life. Everything you do is an enrollment—from the very first conversation, to the sale, and beyond. The key is to always be enrolling.

The Flow

I'm going to share with you a proven system for a successful strategy session. The diagram below shows you the energetic and emotional flow you're aiming for. Mastering this flow is critical so that you aren't turning people off:

1. Set intentions.
2. Get to know the client and build trust.

3. Paint the vision.
4. Identify the perceived obstacles and problems.
5. Unlock the *real* obstacles and problems.
6. Discuss the reality.
7. Share the opportunity.
8. Collect the check.

Step 1: Set Intentions

The most important part of a strategy session is setting intentions from the beginning. I always begin by asking my leads, "What inspired you to have this meeting with me?" Then I share *my* intentions for the meeting. For example, I might say, "My intention for this meeting is to first, understand your vision and the obstacles slowing your success. Second, it is to share with you more about who I am and what I do. Third, if things resonate with you, my intention is to go over finances and share a few options you can invest in to help you achieve your goals faster." It's important to tell them that you will share some things that they can invest in because this prevents people from feeling like there was a bait and switch, which hurts your relationship of trust. Doing it this way actually keeps them from feeling sold to because they are expecting it.

The final part is to then ask them what they are looking for in the meeting with you. From there you can get a good idea of their current mindset and what they are specifically looking for. Now, you have a solid foundation to build on.

Step 2: Build Trust

If this is your first time meeting this person and they have not taken a questionnaire or heard much about you before, you will need to spend a little time getting to know your prospects and building trust. There are several ways you can do this:

- Talk about their family.

- Learn about their business, and ask how they got started.
- Discuss what they do and don't enjoy.
- Ask, "Why do you do what you do?"
- Share your story.

All of these talking points will help you get to know your prospects, discover what makes them tick, and identify what pushes them to thrive. And of course, always remember to share your story. If you don't, that omission will cost you in both money *and* relationships. Your story is the best way to initiate the kind of intimacy and openness you're aiming for in this conversation. However, be careful not to spend more than five or ten minutes on this entire step of building trust. Many people spend way too long here beating around the bush. Just take a few minutes to get to know them, then move on to the next part. They will share much more with you as you go through the next steps.

Step 3: Paint the Vision

Here, you're going to lead them through painting their own vision, and then using it as a tool for inspiration. You can start with something like this: "Let's imagine that three years have gone by, and now we are looking back on those three years. What would have to happen for those to be the most incredible three years of your life? What would have to happen financially, personally, and in business?" You don't have to use this exact script. Everything you're doing should be authentic and coming from *you*, so if this doesn't fit, tweak it until it does. The goal here is that you want to get them to talk. Each time they share something, repeat it back to them, so that they know you heard them, encourage them to elaborate on what they really want.

Once they finish, go even deeper into their vision by asking, "Is there anything else that you feel like needs to happen in those three years for you to feel like it was incredible?" This is important. Sometimes they don't know what their vision is until you walk them through it. You're giving them a gift here, and it's easy to do. Maintain your sincerity. *Listen with the intent to listen.* Don't listen with the intent to sell. The goal is for you to come to understand them. If you can understand them, then you can change their lives. Otherwise, you can't. This isn't about setting your vision aside and holding space for theirs—*your* vision should be to understand them so well that you become best friends. When you know them that well, you will be in a position to intimately serve and to want to serve them.

Yes, your vision is also for them to enroll, but the purpose of that enrollment is to help them. Once you get to that point, there shouldn't be any barriers to their moving forward because they will feel your sincere intention of serving them. At that point, they should feel like, *Of course I'm moving forward with you.* On the rare occasion that your gift really isn't a good fit for that person, then say so. Let them go in the beginning and move on. You can do this if your first priority is to understand them.

Once they've painted a thorough and emotional picture of their three-year vision, paint a picture of their one-year vision. Say, "Now let's imagine that one year has gone by. Which achievement from your three-year vision has to have happened in this *one* year in order for you to honestly say that it has been the most incredible year of your entire life?"

The reason we start with the three-year vision first is to help your clients bypass their fear and doubt that it's possible to achieve what they want in one year. Stepping back to three years helps to disassociate them from their current reality and puts them in a space where they are willing to dream. If you start with the one-year vision, most people will freeze up because they are thinking through the lens of reality. Once they step back enough to be able to frame out the real vision, then you walk them a little closer to that ideal reality by scaling their vision to one year.

Steps 4-5: Identify Perceived Obstacles and Problems, and then Unlock the *Real* Ones

Ask your prospect what could stop them or slow them in creating their one-year vision, and then acknowledge the obstacle and dig further to unlock the *real* obstacles and problems.

Example:

You: "What could stop you from making this million-dollar goal this next year?"

Client: "I don't have the tools and resources."

You: "What tools and resources would you need to achieve your million-dollar goal?" (Let them tell you.) "OK, now let's say you gain these tools and resources. What else might stop or slow you down? What else would keep you from acting on your vision?"

Client: "I don't know. I'd probably achieve it."

You: "How about your mindset? Anything there that could slow you down?"

They will then dive into sharing some emotional barriers or talking about patterns of self-sabotage.

You: "Thank you for sharing. I know it can be hard to confront these problems at times. Is there anything else?"

At this point, the clients may start to squirm because now you're asking them to disclose the real obstacles. You may need to share a story to help them open up. You're getting right into their core. They may start talking about difficult relationships that are blocking them, or their fear of success, or limiting beliefs surrounding money. Their real problems and obstacles are going to come out. You're continuing to gently prod them to go deeper, and you're listening. Listening is the key. Don't push, don't pull. Ask guiding questions and listen. Some people get right to it. For others, you may have to just go deeper with them.

You: "Let's be real. Your time is valuable. My time is valuable. What is *really* stopping you? You have this vision of XYZ, and I realize the tools and resources might be a part of why you don't have it yet, but there's something deeper, isn't there? This is kind of like what I went through...."

Here, you are positioned to share your stories to help diffuse some of their obstacles and fears. Share a story from your own life when you had deep blocks stopping you from manifesting your vision. Share your stories in response to their feelings as a way to diffuse and to validate, or share your stories in order to initiate their sharing. Your openness and vulnerability will invite theirs.

If you can't see yourself taking someone through this discovery process, then you need to ask yourself what you might be afraid of. *You* may have some blocks. What's keeping you from being able to communicate about any subject with any human? Whether it's money, family, personal struggles—you name it. If you feel yourself seizing up on anything, you have to take inventory of your own blocks and remove them. The whole point here is to become free so you can help other people become free.

Step 6: Discuss the Reality

Once you uncover the real problems and obstacles, discuss them. Bring your clients to a place where they have to face those problems and see them for what they are. This allows them to be honest with themselves about where they are, which is the first step in recognizing the way out. Going there will be a short journey because they've already been there their whole lives. However, now you're going to turn a light on for them so they can be aware. This can be an uncomfortable step for your clients. However, you're going to do it because you care about them. This is what is necessary for them to be able to recognize the solution you hold that will allow them to break free of that place.

Here are some questions that can take you deeper and deeper into this place of reality:

- Where else have you seen patterns of these same problems and obstacles showing up in your life?
- On a scale of one to ten, how hard have you tried to overcome them? (If they say anything other than an eight, nine, or ten, it's usually a three or four. Sixes and sevens are fours in disguise.)
- What number do you think you have to be at in order to achieve this?
- What's kept your effort from being that number? (Make sure that you're creating a safe place of non-judgment so they can open up here.)
- If you could change this, what would that do for your life?
- How much do you want to change?
- Are you fully committed to doing whatever it takes to overcome this? On a scale of zero to ten, ten being the

top priority and zero being none at all, how committed are you to *yourself?* Up to this point, everything—every question, every comment, every story—has been about getting them to open up and talk to you. Once they are in a place where they are acknowledging, and even feeling the pain of being stuck, they are ready to commit to move forward.

Step 7: Share the Opportunity

Once they are fully committed to take action to change, you can share the opportunities with them. A great way to segue into that is to say something like, "Now that we have talked about what you want and how committed you are, would you like to see some things I have that you can get plugged in to in order to achieve XYZ faster?" If they say yes, then you can say, "Let's dive into your financial situation so I know what is the best fit for you." You should already have an idea of where they are financially from asking about their vision and obstacles, but now you're getting even more getting specific.

I often share something like this: "I have packages ranging from a couple hundred dollars to sixty thousand dollars. Based on what you want, and I have an idea of what it will take, I want to know how much money you have to invest in achieving XYZ. That way we can make the best fit. You may have to share a story here if people are shy about opening up about money. Then continue, asking specific questions about how much is in their banking or savings accounts and their 401k, whether they use credit cards or loans, etc. Then you can share whatever is the opportunity that fits that person perfectly. This is where your package comes in to play. The package you built in the last chapter is your blueprint that outlines the solutions to their problems, and leverages you as the person most qualified to solve them. You will share your structure of what it is you're actually selling. **This is the first time in your strategy session that you are discussing your offering.** Period.

You will share in detail only one to two steps of your package. Share the ones that are most appropriate to their situation, based on what they've shared with you. Show them how to apply those steps for immediate results. Step up your excitement and speak as if they are already doing it. Once shared, go over the structure of the rest of your program and how they can access it. Talk about what it will be like working with you. Sound excited about your package; this is important. Have you ever talked to someone who isn't excited about what they're sharing? They speak in a monotone, and you're just nodding off while you listen. If you want them to emotionally engage with your product, you have to emotionally engage them in the conversation. Be excited about your program and about the kind of life they are so close to living. Otherwise it's as if you're asking for their permission to like it. You're seeking approval. If you have that attitude, you will get rejected and rejected and rejected.

The real question is whether *you* believe in your message.

If you do, and you know it will change lives and you care about the people you're trying to help, you will be passionate about it—and you should be. If you're not the passionate type, then you need to be intense. Personally, I get a little crazy because I'm a passionate person. I used to be afraid of that. Now I own it. I used to intentionally restrain that part of myself because I was afraid of emotion due to pornography and my interpretations of the divorces my parents went through. I was afraid to communicate my passion because I was afraid I was going to hurt someone. That passion and that intensity turned inward and was channeled into addiction, which hurt me. When I finally forgave myself and let go of that fear, I was able to give myself permission to play and be passionate about my message.

Step Eight: Collect the Check

By the time you ask your clients to make an investment, you must have covered these five bases:

- Want: You've validated what they want most.
- Feel: They are excited, ready, and in agreement.
- Know: They know at least three benefits they'll receive by working with you.
- Have: They know what results they will have as a result of working with you.
- Do: They know what to do to get from point A to B (i.e. fill out papers, sign a check, etc.)

Fifteen percent of the people you talk to will happily hand you a check simply because you helped them dream. The other 85 percent will need you to take them through the cost of inaction versus the cost of action, or COI vs. COA. You don't need to use this all the time, but it does help someone become more aware if it really has been costing them a lot over the years. Most people don't take the time to count it up, so they continue living in the pain.

For example, let's say you're coaching someone on how to make money, and they say they want to make $1,000,000 in three years, and $500,000 in the first year. However, right now they're only making about $80,000 a year. How much is it going to cost them if they don't take action right now to change things, so they stay stuck at $80,000? It will cost them $420,000 in the next year. Walk them step by step through this scenario. "If you don't change anything, that's what it's going to cost you in real dollars, in addition to the frustration, energy, and pain you can't put a price on." Then, you compare that cost to the cost of your program. "So, the cost of my program, the cost of *action*, is $10,000. What's $10,000 compared to $420,000? The cost of inaction is substantially more than the cost of action, and you're still going to net a $410,000 gain." It is also good to point out what it has cost them to not take action in previous year.

If you are teaching or coaching someone about things other than money, like health or relationships, you can still use this method by substituting another source of pain in place of money. Continue to inspire them in their goals and dreams by helping them really want to change and find real solutions.

You can create more value by doing some of the following:

- Mention a similar product or service that is more expensive than yours. This positions yours to be a good value. Just don't make the margin so grossly high that it makes your package look inferior.

- Share your regular price—what the investment would be if some random stranger came to you to buy it.

- Offer a "Today Only" price. However, be honest about it. Don't say it's a limited-time offer if it isn't. If you say it's going to be a different price the next day, and then they call you the next day and ask for it, hold to your boundary. Give it to them for the price you said you would the next day. This helps them stay accountable. Keep your commitments, which will help them keep theirs.

- Offer a payment plan. For example, if you have an $8,000 package, you can offer a payment plan of nine $1,000 payments, or just one payment of $8,000 for a savings of $1,000. The payment plan can be modified depending on the size of the down payment.

- Add bonuses to your main offer for taking action now. This motivates people to do it now instead of waiting, since waiting creates an opportunity for their negative thinking to set back in.

Once you've worked out the terms of payment, the final part of the sale is to set expectations and give a clear picture of what to do next. Tell them exactly how to make their payment, down to whom the check needs to be made out to, and schedule your first appointment. Be very thorough.

Objections

If clients aren't taking action at this point, it's because there is still some lingering confusion. Your job is to help them get unconfused. In order to do that, you need to have clarity about what's really being communicated when they express their concerns and hesitations. What they say and what they mean may be two totally different things.

Here are some examples of the false objections you might hear:

- I don't have enough time.
- I don't have enough money, or it's too expensive.
- I have to talk to my spouse.
- I need to think about it/pray about it.
- Now isn't the right time.

What they're *really* saying is:

- I don't trust you yet.
- I don't believe in myself to do it, or I am scared to fail.
- I am unclear about what it is I am receiving or how we will start.
- I am unsure how this solves my problems.
- I have some unanswered questions.
- I need you to ask me more questions so I can figure out what I really need.

If someone is not taking action when it is clearly a priority for them to do so, these are the only reasons why. So, I just ask more questions. "What more do you need to know before getting started today? What is it that's keeping you from moving forward? Is it money, time, or fear? Tell me about it. The best time to talk is right now. So, let's talk." Don't just say, "Do you have any questions?" because they'll just say no. You have to guide them through this process. It takes some courage and guts on your part, but also some caring kindness. You have to be bold, but not overbearing. You are challenging their limiting beliefs, but you don't want them to feel like you're challenging them as a person. You will use your stories to help diffuse their objections and concerns. You will also use good logic.

For example, in addition to sharing my money story, here are some ways I might diffuse the money objection:

- "If money and time were not an obstacle, would you be interested in my program?"
- "Do you not have any money at all, or is it that you do not have any extra money in your budget for this?"
- "If your spouse were here, what would s/he say? Would you like to get on a call with your spouse right now so we can chat?"
- Walk them through a visualization: "Let's say you have an uncle who lives in Mexico. He passes away and leaves you $15,000. The only catch is that you have to fly to Mexico to get it in person. Otherwise, you can't have it. You are guaranteed $15,000 on the other end of your trip. However, it's going to cost you $4,000 to go get it—and you don't have that $4,000. What are you going to do? You only have one week to claim the money." I encourage them to do whatever it takes. If they have to get a loan, they're not going into debt— they're making an investment in their business.

- Walk them through real scenarios in which they can make it happen. Create a doable plan of action, and talk them through it as a visualization so that they can see themselves creating the money to make it happen and benefiting from the outcome of doing so.
- I teach the difference in mindset between the poor, the middle class, and the rich:
  - Poor mindset: they don't budget and don't invest.
  - Middle-class mindset: they budget, and they only put money toward things that are important to them. They don't go outside of their budget otherwise.
  - Rich mindset: They invest in opportunity. Period. They say, "Hey, if there's an opportunity that will create more money for me, I'm going to invest and make it happen—borrow it, move it, put it over there, and make it happen."

These are some examples on how to address the money objection, but you can modify any one of them to fit any objection. I specifically discussed the money objection because that is the one you're going to hear the most often, and the one you personally are most likely going to have to overcome. (We'll talk more about that in the next chapter.)

Whatever the objections are, just recognize them as a door you have to walk through to get to your final destination. Remember, the key here is to absolutely **know what you want**. That will give you an innate sense of direction, regardless of any objections that try to derail you. Your client should hear the price within the first thirty minutes of the strategy session, and *then* the real dance begins—not because you have to talk them into giving you their money, but because they may not be accustomed to making investments in themselves. If you have done your job and shown up with an authentic and sincere desire to help them, you have to recognize that walking them through objectives is not about high-pressure sales. It's about being their guide through unfamiliar territory. Stay with them until you arrive at the destination. Expect to make a call to action at least three to five times. Once they decide to move forward, get them excited about their decisions and congratulate them.

Top Six Mistakes to Avoid

If your client doesn't enroll, it's likely because of one of the following reasons:

- You didn't allow them to dream and see their vision.
- You only made a call to action once or twice.
- You gave them more than a day to think about it without seeing what they needed.
- You let them talk to their spouse, instead of allowing you to be the one to outline the package to the spouse.
- You gave it to them for free because you felt sorry for them.
- The conversation ended with unsaid words or feelings.

There are rare occasions that you end up talking with someone who really isn't a good fit for your program. In that event, don't try to cram a square peg into a round hole. Release them, but be sure to ask for a referral before you do.

Keep in mind that there is going to be a learning curve to the strategy session. Don't get discouraged if you bomb your first round of these. That isn't you failing. It's you practicing. Keep an abundant mindset. Realize that there are always more chances to do better. There will always be a next time—but always be learning from *this* time.

Follow Up

If you leave the session without a check, but you know they are still interested in what you have to offer, make sure you schedule a follow up. Follow up is not bugging them. Follow up is caring about them. There is power in follow-ups. The biggest mistake people make is failing to follow up because they assume people aren't interested, when in reality, they're thinking. They just need someone to help them take action. If you feel as if you're bugging them, then you feel as if you're selling them. However, if you feel as if your message could change their lives, and you don't follow up, what kind of friend are you? Some people really just need a few conversations and that's OK. Others, though, are people who may be trapped in a cycle of fear, worry, or limiting beliefs, and they are suffering. You choose to follow up because you recognize that you have a way to help them. Your message can change their lives and help them achieve their goals. You don't want to share your gift in a way that you're pushing it on them, but if you know you can help them change their lives, do it.

Imagine you have a beautiful banquet of food, and someone you know is starving. You tell them all about this beautiful meal. They respond by telling you they are hungry and malnourished. You ask, "Would you like to eat this?"

"Well, I'm not quite sure," they say.

Would you take the food away because you don't want to push it on them? Absolutely not. Instead you'd say, "Why don't you want to eat this beautiful food? Maybe I didn't describe it in enough detail." Then you go on to describe the food more thoroughly. You point out their favorite food, you talk about the smells and the rich flavors, and you paint a picture of how it will feel for their stomach to finally be full. Is that a bad thing to do? Does that feel pushy? If you have a beautiful banquet to share with someone who is dying, is it wrong to follow up with that person until they eat? *If it feels like it is wrong, you need to increase your personal sense of value.* Recognize how powerful your message is. If you can help them, and you don't, then shame on you. Love them enough to follow up. Care enough to give them this banquet.

If you feel as if you aren't communicating your message well, or if you aren't sure about your own intentions, ask yourself what is holding you back. You must believe in yourself before someone else can capture the vision enough to purchase your package. Don't base your value on whether someone is willing to exchange money for it. It has nothing to do with that. Don't wait for someone to give you permission to feel good about your gift. Own the value of your gift, and then others will catch on.

If you're not valuing yourself now, you will end up talking to all the wrong people, which are the people you feel comfortable talking to. These are most likely people who are in lower energy and financial brackets. If you want to find the right people, talk to people who are more successful than you—the people who scare you. When you want to change, your energy will pull the people who are also changing, and repel the people who aren't. You have to let go of the people who are content to stay stuck. You are here to *harvest* the people who are ready, not change the ones who aren't.

For me strategy sessions are the most lifechanging conversations on the planet. At first, I was afraid of having one because I didn't want to be "sold to." However, as I embraced what I feared and avoided, I was able to see that a lot of the hesitation I felt was affecting how I treated people, especially potential clients. I had old, negative emotions that were slowing my success. Going through a strategy session helped me get clear on my purpose and mission, and it helped me find the strength to commit to work on myself and master my craft. I want to invite those of you who feel called to experience this yourself to go to enroll-mentmasters.com/ss and schedule a strategy session. See for yourself. If you are looking to get 10 times the clarity and direction, if you are ready to go to the next level, and especially if you need to be called out on some things—stop right now and go schedule your session. That is called taking action.

CHAPTER TEN
Money

As you start practicing the strategy session, the biggest and most common block you're going to hit is money. This is true both for you and your clients. I personally believe the biggest test on this planet is money. Can you be good enough, can you be who you are supposed to be, and can you serve your Higher Power and those around you without fear of money? The test is whether you will master the money mindset instead of letting money master you.

The reason this test is so hard is because money is not just money. It is the exchange for everything. People exchange their time—the absolute fabric of their lives—for money. You can understand why many of us associate money with life. Even before our currency consisted of paper money and coins, we had a system of exchange for everything that money embodies today. This currency understandably represents food, shelter, and freedom to do the activities that you want to do. The energy behind money is sacrifice, blood, sweat, and tears. Your attitudes and beliefs about money are manifest in every monetary transaction you make.

I see this with my own clients. If people want to pay only a little bit, then they are willing to invest only a little energy into changing. This means they aren't sure if the process will work, they're afraid of something, or they don't feel worthy enough to make a greater investment into themselves. I interpret a world of meaning from their willingness, or unwillingness, to financially enroll. I sit across from people during my strategy sessions and see these realities working their way through their hearts and minds, then out through their objections and decisions. Then I have to make a decision. Do I try to save them? Or do I teach them?

Savioritis

For a long time, I had a condition called Savioritis—meaning I wanted to save everyone. It started when I was a kid going through my parents' multiple divorces. I felt as if I had to save my mom from pain. In an effort to free her, I tried to take all of her burdens and load them onto myself instead. As I grew up, I took on this same role in my other relationships, too—always trying to save others from pain by taking it on myself. I was trying to be everyone's Savior. I consistently volunteered myself to be the sacrifice. I went through a lot of anguish before I realized this was not saving anyone, and I was destroying myself in the process.

We are not here to save people. That's already been taken care of by Someone else. So, when you step into the, "I have to save people" mode, you attract the people who are looking to be saved, and you all end up drowning. If you really want to help people, help them see how valuable they are and teach them to fish instead of giving them fish. Teach them to *do* instead of *doing* for them. Teach them to *become* instead of *being* for them.

I've had to learn this lesson time and again. I attracted only low-paying clients who had no money for far too long. These were people I could clearly see needed help, so I would step in and try to save them in spite of their inability to pay. Then none of us had any money. I depleted myself and my resources by giving to them, and I felt horrible. I became angry with them and angry with myself. I kept asking, "What am I doing? Why do I keep doing this?" Then I started noticing people who were serving and helping those who had money to pay for services. They served with sincerity, kindness, and passion, and they were living in abundance.

I knew I had to change.

First, I had to let go of trying to save people. I repeat: *You are not here to save people.* You are here to serve and love—and loving others means helping them to be self-sufficient and to change. If someone wants my gift, but they don't have enough money, I immediately recognize that they have some sort of negative emotion or thought that is blocking their abundance. Instead of taking it on personally, I simply note that they don't have enough and say, "Oh, you don't have enough. How long has that been going on? A few years? Your whole life? Would you like to change that? Isn't it about time that you step out of that so you can be abundant?" I no longer what to save them. Instead, I want to teach them and to help them believe in themselves enough to invest and do something different so they can get into a higher energy level and attract more to their lives.

So, I did two things:

1. I created some alternative low-end products that allowed people to invest only a few hundred dollars if what I offered wasn't a fit financially.

2. I no longer spent thirty minutes to an hour with people who couldn't afford it. I quickly said, "Hey, if you want to have a strategy session, I require a credit card number. If you don't show up, I'm going to charge it for $500 because my time is valuable, and so is yours." This weeded out the people who were scared of $500—people who could still hop on to one of my lower-priced classes.

In this way, I'm teaching them, but not saving them. Instead of spending two to three hours trying to change them, I'm quickly guiding them to resources they can use to change themselves. That takes the responsibility off of me. I still love them and want to help them, but I no longer sacrifice my value in order to artificially prop up theirs.

When I first decided to set these boundaries and make these shifts, the next five people I attracted were people who couldn't afford my higher package. I was tested. That boundary triggered a lot of emotions inside of me. I had to work through them in order to get my value up and be able to say, "No, I'm worth it. These people need me to help them, and this is the best way I can do that." I held my ground, and I called on my Higher Power to help me through that change.

Now, when people come into my life, I am straight up with them, and I ask early into our conversations where they are financially. This protects both my time and theirs. If I'm talking to people who don't have that mindset yet, I steer them toward my lower-paid classes. This allows me to work exclusively with people who have money or are willing to take intelligent risks, who want help, and who recognize the value of exchanging money for that help. I teach them about value—about valuing themselves, their families, and their Higher Power—and about how value will create the impact they desire.

Money mindset is in the fabric of all of this.

How you value yourself is a big part of this whole money mindset. Money is a currency, and so is your time. What do you feel you deserve? Do you feel as if you need to work hard and suffer before you get your money? Or do you feel you are a divine being who is worthy of abundance? If you really believe that you are a divine being, then you're not going to settle for giving all of your time and effort—basically, your *own* life—for the sake of people who say they can't pay you. If you value yourself, and if you save your time for those who are committed to do what it takes to change, you'll have more time to serve more people. If you're always working for people who say they can't pay you, then you have no energy left to do what you're on the planet to accomplish. The truth of the matter is that anyone can pay for anything on this planet. There really is an abundance on this earth. Those with limiting fears just don't see the opportunities and resources around them.

So, how do you feel about yourself, and what do you actually deserve? If you are committed to doing whatever your Higher Power wants you to do, and having everything He wants for you, then realize that He thinks you're awesome. If you mirror that value for yourself, then you'll hold to it and attract the people who can pay you, which will then allow you to have the resources to serve those who can't.

Once you make this shift, you're still going to give free strategy sessions—and you'll start out still giving free strategy sessions with people who can't afford you. You're going to be tested. You'll still be sitting down and having conversations with people who don't have money as long as that's where your energy is focused. Once you shift that, people with higher energy will be attracted to you. If you want to increase the value of your strategy session, then do something as I do with the credit card numbers. It will manifest their blocks and help you sift through people so you don't end up doing strategy sessions with people who claim they can't afford you or those who aren't committed to change. If you value yourself, people value you and they show up. Your clients' objections or limitations are reflections of your personal doubts and fears. Understand this and the game becomes transformational.

Staying Neutral

There was a time in my life when I had just forty-nine cents in my bank account and no income coming in. I was drowning in school debts with no way to pay for them, or anything else for that matter. I felt miserable. I was dating Emily (now my wife) at the time, and I shared with her my worries by posing a hypothetical situation that was actually mine so she wouldn't know how bad off I was.

I said, "Having only forty-nine cents in your bank account would make anyone feel poor and worried."

Emily looked at me like I was crazy and said something that changed my life. She said, "The real test, Tyler, is whether you can feel rich with just forty-nine in your account."

My immediate thought was, "Heck, no! Give me money, and I will feel rich."

She looked at me even more deeply and repeated her thoughts. "The test isn't how much is in the account, but whether you can become rich no matter what your circumstance."

I paused, then decided right then and there that I was rich. I no longer wanted to be a slave to money.

In order to master this money mindset, you have to feel completely neutral about money. If thoughts of money—having it, not having it, asking for it, giving it away, anything at all pertaining to money—trigger negative emotions and thoughts for you, that's an indicator that you have some issues to work on. In order to track that, I'm going to sit you down with money and ask you to explore what's going on inside of you. Write down the emotions that come to you during this exercise.

What comes to your mind when you see a $1 bill? Easy come, easy go, right? This power to purchase has a different energy than a $2 bill. Do you feel the difference in energy inside you, or is it about the same?

Now look at a $5 bill. Is it different? Does it have the same energy to it? It's a higher energy, right?

How about a $10 bill? What emotions come up?

Now a $20 bill. If someone handed you a $20 bill, would that be different than a $1 bill?

What if someone handed you a $50 bill? What would be going on in your mind and with your feelings? What about $100?

What about a $500 bill? (These are kind of rare, but they do exist.) What would happen? What would you feel? What thoughts or emotions would you have? How would you feel?

What about a $1,000 bill? What happens? Is it different than the $500 bill? If so, how much different?

What about $5,000? What would go on inside of your heart and mind if this amount of money suddenly came your way? Write down the emotions this stirs in you.

$10,000?

$100,000?
$1,000,000?
Here is the test. Can you feel just as excited, fulfilled, peace-ful, and ready to serve your Higher Power with just forty-nine cents in your account as you do when you receive $1,000,000? That's the test. Imagine while you're standing in the grocery line, someone hands you a dollar, and you erupt into celebration. People would think you're crazy, but why don't you have that excitement? Why does a dollar not make you feel as safe as $1,000,000?

Why do you let the money dictate your emotions when the emotions are inside of you? If you can master your thoughts and emotions—that energy inside of you—then it won't matter if you have millions of dollars or no money at all. You'll be just as happy, just as safe, just as passionate, driven, caring, giving, and kind. All of those feelings that come to the surface when you're thinking about $1,000,000 all come from inside of you. You can get to a place where *you* are calling forth those feelings, inde-pendent of the numbers in your bank account. You don't need money to be happy. You can be happy because of your own sense of value. If your happiness is tied to money, then whom are you serving? Money or God? If you truly served your Higher Power, then your happiness would come from the Source, *not* money. If you are truly serving your Source and the people around you, then your feelings will have zero dependence on the amount of cash you have.

I hope you're starting to see why it's so important to get to a place where your energy surrounding money is neutral and void of triggers. Once you stop worrying about money, it will come more easily. The worry is creating a barrier of negative energy that is repelling it. Whether you feel worthy of high-pay-ing clients is going to frame your ability to ask them to enroll. If you are consumed by a fear that there isn't enough money coming to you, that fear will cripple your ability to put your clients' needs first, making it impossible to have authentic conversations and successful strategy sessions. The exchange of money is neutral. You ask, and you receive. Everything else—all of these fears, insecurities, and misconceptions about money—just creates a barrier to the exchange. However, once you can be neutral, and once you can see the exchange for the simple transaction that it is, the barriers are gone, and the transaction will happen with ease.

Being neutral will also increase your gratitude. When I receive a check for $20, I do the same money dance I do when I receive a check for $50,000. I'm showing the Universe that I'm grateful for everything that flows to me. A gift is a gift. Don't size it up and dismiss it because it's not big enough. It's not about the quantity—it's about receiving. I want to be a good receiver so that I can be a good giver. So, when I get paid $20, yes, I will be happy and rejoice. If I don't get paid, I will still be happy and rejoice because I recognize my value is far beyond the numbers in my bank account. As I maintain this neutrality and gratitude, I am able to maintain peace and opportunity.

Money is Just Energy

The first step in neutralizing your thoughts and feelings surrounding money is to see it for what it is and to dissociate it from the things that it is not. The goal here is to hone in on answering the question, *What is money?* What is this substance that you think about day in and day out? What is this currency that you need in order to live? More important, how can you master it so that you're capable of receiving it in abundance? How can you make a shift so that you feel confident and good about asking people to enroll at a high price point?

In order to answer these questions, we have to go back to Einstein's Theory of Relativity, $E=mc^2$. We covered that in length in the second chapter. Understanding this equation will unlock your ability to master the money mindset. Remember that there is a direct correlation between the amount of energy in the formula and the resulting amount of mass. This is true when we put in money for mass—and it's also true when we put in your negative thoughts, emotions, and beliefs for mass. As you increase your energy investment, you will increase your results, which is a measurement of the amount of matter present. The reverse is also true. As you decrease your energy investment, you will also decrease your resulting mass.

We previously established that thoughts have matter, and I shared with you the following diagram, which demonstrated that your energy is comprised of your thoughts, emotions, and actions. Your thoughts create emotions, which create your actions, which produce your results (your mass).

When we talk about energy, it's important to note that there are two different types of energy; positive and negative. This is easy to demonstrate. If you have a thought about hatred and feel the emotion of loathing someone, that energy is obviously different from thoughts of love and peace. Negative thoughts produce negative emotions; positive thoughts produce positive emotions. Emotion is a measure of energy in motion in your heart, whether it is positive or negative. We can see that everything in nature has positives and negatives. Ions, protons, electrons, everything, as these are the building blocks of our world. Everything has a charge so that it can attract or repulse. That's what creates flow, or life.

When you have a negative thought such as, *I hate this person*, that thought is sending a lower, slower frequency than that of a positive thought. Positive thoughts have higher, faster frequencies—a higher vibration. As such, positive frequencies create more movement, and this movement is necessary for creation. Therefore, higher frequencies have a stronger power to create.

Now, we're going to go into this farther as it pertains to money.

Money has mass, and it is therefore a product of energy, which is a product of thoughts, emotions, and actions—whether positive or negative. The value of one dollar is a measure of its mass, and is therefore a measurement of mass itself. One hundred dollars is also a measure of mass. So is one thousand dollars, ten thousand dollars, one hundred thousand dollars, one million dollars, and so on. According to Einstein's law, the amount of mass is a reflection of the energy investment. So, if I'm not creating the money I want, then it just shows that the frequency of my life is different than the frequency of the money.

Do you understand what I'm saying?

Scientifically, the amount of money you have is a reflection of the energy and vibration you're investing in its creation. Your positive thoughts count. So do your negative thoughts. Some of those negative thoughts may include fears about asking for money or feeling as if you're asking for too much money. You may be concerned that having too much money will make the IRS target you. Perhaps you feel selfish when you require an exchange of money for your time. You may feel crippled by your lack of money, as if you are trapped in a cycle of not enough. All of these feelings create an energy that directly affects the mass of the money in your life. The sum of your energy investment *is* the amount of money you have.

The good news is that these numbers are fluid, and they can easily be manipulated.

Take Immediate Action

Let's take a minute and find out where you are on this spectrum, so you can get an honest perception of how far you need to move your needle. What is money to *you*? Set a timer for five minutes, and write down everything that comes to your mind when you think about money—the good, the bad, and the ugly. What does it mean to you? How do you react to having it or not having it? What feelings does it trigger? What does it symbolize? Write for the entire five minutes. If you get stuck, ask more questions to keep your juices flowing.

The Apple is Close to its Tree

Now, look over what you just wrote down. Where did these thoughts, feelings, and beliefs come from? We receive a lot of our ideas and beliefs about money from the people who raised us. Each family has a unique culture, and part of that culture revolves around money.

When I was growing up, my parents struggled with finances. There were times when we had plenty, and there were times when we didn't. My dad came from a family that really struggled financially. When he was twelve, he went out on his own to create money and provide for himself. He knew he had to work hard to make a living, and if he didn't then he didn't feel worthy. Once he had the money, though, he was comfortable spending it because he had the belief that there was always more money at the other end of more work; it came and it went, and it always would.

My mom was different. She grew up in a family that struggled and budgeted and wouldn't spend on anything unless there was a need. She grew up very thrifty with a family culture of only buying absolute necessities and never spending outside the budget.

Obviously, these two individuals had very different ideas and beliefs around money. When they established a family of their own, they then merged their two money energies together and created an entirely new creature altogether. Growing up, I learned several different things. My dad taught me that I had to work hard and physically exhaust myself to get paid. I also learned from him that money could come easily, but I had to work for it and go the extra mile to earn that extra buck. On the one hand, he showed me that I could be generous and give money away, and on the other hand, that I could give myself permission to do and to buy the things I wanted to do and to buy. My mother taught me to save every penny, and that if I didn't need something I shouldn't buy it. I also learned from her that I should first try to find what I needed at the thrift store. If I could buy something used for one dollar, there was no reason to go pay ten dollars for the same thing new somewhere else.

Those were my thoughts and emotions around money, even though my parents never sat me down and intentionally taught me these values. As a family, we didn't talk about money. Any time I heard my parents talking about it was usually because they were arguing over its lack, stressing over bills that weren't getting paid, or worried over extra expenses when appliances, cars, or the other necessities of life broke down. The dialogue was generally negative or avoided completely. That was my training.

What emotions and thoughts about money did I inherit? What energy and frequency were planted inside of me? I merged the two thoughts of being thrifty and scarce, and being abundant and overspending. I became someone who would work really hard and not spend a dime until I found something that was truly worth the expense. I believed that if I didn't work until I was physically exhausted, I didn't deserve money or that I was taking advantage of someone. This created a major block to being able to receive money with ease. I had a hard time valuing my gifts enough to expect to be paid well for them. In order to feel worthy of payment, I had to deplete all of my energy and effort in the exchange, which limited the number of people I was able to serve. I was a slave to money and felt like a victim of it. It definitely symbolized blood, sweat, and tears for me, so it was hard to invest it back into myself. If an opportunity came my way, I would make a decision based on whether I could afford it instead of whether it was the right thing to do.

All of this created a threshold to abundance that seemed impossible to penetrate. I had to make a massive and sustained investment of energy to reform these negative thoughts and emotions into positive ones.

What did *you* learn growing up? What thoughts and emotions were transferred to you as part of your family's culture? Some of them could have been positive and abundant—and some of them were likely not so positive.

I hope you can see the reality of this transfer of energy and look at it without judgement. It just is what it is. And whatever it is doesn't have to stay that way. Remember that energy, money, thoughts, and beliefs—these are all fluid. Energy can't be created or destroyed, but it *can* be changed. You can't create new energy, but you can take old, negative energy and reshape it into positive and abundant energy.

Take Immediate Action

Now you're going to slow down your negative thoughts and emotions so you can intentionally change them to positives. Remember, energy is just mass sped up really fast. So, as you slow down your negative thoughts and emotions, you are already reducing the amount of energy being wasted on them. I'm going to take you through a process of transformation and of release that will raise your frequency and vibration so that you can physically increase the mass of your money. Here are the steps:

1. Get out a piece of paper and a pen. Think of your mom, dad, or someone close to you that has affected your value and money mindset. You're not blaming them—you're just being honest about your interpretation of their contribution to your mindset up to this point.

2. Write, "I have negative feelings/thoughts about money from [that person] because...." Then set a timer for eight minutes and write three separate paragraphs, or reasons. Start each paragraph with the same sentence above. Write whatever comes to your mind. You're training your subconscious to show you the blocks so you can clear them. Hopefully you're going to have some "Aha!" moments here— some real eye openers about how and why you regard money the way you do.

3. Go to a room where you are alone and read the whole paper *aloud*. Reading it aloud is important, based on the principle of $E=mc^2$, because this slows it down so you can acknowledge and manage them.

4. After you've read it, ask aloud for forgiveness from three people:
   a. Your Higher Power: "Please forgive me for having these feelings and not getting rid of them sooner."

b. Yourself: "I forgive myself for having these feelings and acting on them and not forgiving myself sooner."

c. The person you named in this exercise: "I forgive my mom for having these negative beliefs and modeling them."

As you ask for forgiveness, you're being submissive, which will open your heart and open you to change. You're not blaming anyone; you're forgiving them. More than anything else, a hard heart and a closed mind are what will stop you from sharing your passion. This process immediately unravels the negative bond and sets your heart and mind free so you can love, accept, and forgive.

5. Finally, tear up the piece of paper or burn it—just get rid of it.

I suggest doing this exercise several times, and often. You will discover something new each time. If you do this two days from now, new things are going to come up because your subconscious is saying, "Oh you want to get rid of this? Here's more!" Going back to the Principle of Flow, you will have more space for new and better beliefs and emotions as you release the ones that have been shaping you up to this point.

If you want some additional resources on how you can recalibrate your perspective on money, I recommend reading *Jack Rabbit Factor*, by my good friend Leslie Householder. It's a very engaging story that teaches you about how to rethink and attract money in your life, which is exactly what it did for me. If you want a more hands-on experience, come to our four-day intensive training on money mindsets called Impact 2 Income.

Once you are neutral about money, you are able to invest your entire focus on your mission, passion, and helping people change. This will massively increase the opportunities in your life, and subsequently increase your income. Personally, I've found that when I worry about not having enough, it is because I have forgotten my God—the true Source of all things. If I worry, it's because I've allowed my life to be dictated by fear instead of faith.

However, once I recalibrate myself so that I am serving only Him, and I know He is my boss, then I know that He will pro- vide for me. He will give me enough. He will give me plenty. The first step to that is to recognize who or what you're serving, and then to adjust accordingly. You'll go in and out of that assurance. It can be a struggle not to allow money, or the lack thereof, to change your emotions. However, I can attest to the fact that once your state is no longer dictated by numbers, you will be able to live more fully in the state of love, passion, service, and peace that you're striving for, and leave a blazing path for others to follow.

CHAPTER ELEVEN
Conclusion

Thank you for taking this ride with me. This is where I get off, but your journey has only just begun. You will find that reading about the Enrollment Effect is a very different experience than experiencing the Enrollment Effect. Now comes the part where you have to actually *do it*. Don't make the mistake of waiting to apply these principles—do it *right now*. Find an event and start practicing immediately. Expect a learning curve, and don't call "failure" when it's not failure at all. It's just practice. The faster you get out there and start practicing, the sooner you will be able to harness the full power of the Enrollment Effect by mastering the skills and emotions necessary to break through and live life by design.

One of the biggest breakthroughs I have seen the people I work with experience comes from a four-day event called *Connect: Master The One To One*. My wife and I facilitate this event to help our clients cut years off the learning curve in their business. During this event we attempt to cover all of the principles you are learning in this book. It is one thing to read about a concept, and it is another to experience it hands on. Imagine if you could take 40 years of struggle and eliminate it in four days. That is my intention at our events.

By the time someone goes through the four days they:

1) Connect with others, money, and their Higher Power in deeper ways.
2) Build and refine their package at the event.

3) Practice sharing stories with like-minded people.
4) Practice the strategy session with live people who give feedback.
5) Actually sell your product or service to the group.
6) Go through emotional tools to help you rid yourself of old negative blocks.

By the time people finish, they are exhausted from changing so fast, they're inspired to live their message, and they have grown their clientele base and developed sales skills all at the same time. Many people make back the money they invested to attend the event by the time the event is over. If you would like to check out what our event is like and what others have experienced, go to enrollmentmasters.com/connect.

We have seen people literally go from food stamps to creating over 40k in a month after what they learned and applied at the event. Go check it out right now.

If you have questions or would like a discount promo price, email support@thefreedomcatalyst.com and mention that you found this invitation in my book. It's my gift to you for reading the whole book.

Patience and Persistence

In order to continue this journey, you need to live the principles of patience and persistence. You need to apply these for your own success, and also for the success of the people you want to reach. As you live these principles, you will be able to model them for others. You will be the success story you want to be, and a seasoned veteran of victory over perceived obstacles.

This is what sets people that have success stories apart from people who don't.

If you have something on your vision board that's taking a long time, stay persistent and I promise it will work. Remember the Law of Gestation—that there is a period of time necessary for your dreams to manifest after they are planted. Be patient during the growing season. For example, in 2013, I was part of some networking companies, and I set the goal to make six figures by a certain time. This was completely new to me. I didn't even know what six figures looked like. I set the intention to achieve that goal through a networking company because that's the only path I could conceive of that would lead me there. However, my heart wasn't in it. The more I worked, the more I felt I wasn't driven. I wanted to change my focus. I prayed and meditated, and I felt like I needed to keep the goal, but change the path—not because I was afraid, but because I wanted to follow the clues my heart was giving me.

It was still a tough decision. I was barely making ends meet and I wasn't experiencing a lot of success. However, I knew where I wanted to go so I kept moving and taking inspired action, month after month. I kept working at it until, finally, I started creating some results, generating income, and seeing people's lives change. I held to my vision and stayed persistent. In less than a year, I went from creating less than $1,000 a month, to clearing my first six figures. Even though I didn't get there on the path I initially thought would take me there, I was firm in where I wanted to go so the path unraveled before me. I was open enough to change that I was still able to take the fastest route possible.

It's important to allow yourself that same fudge factor so you can adapt when necessary. You're always going to be making adjustments and improvements to your path. However, if you want to fast-track your transformation and reduce the amount of time you're stuck in trial and error, reach out and get plugged in to our live events, coaching programs, or any of our courses designed to take you to the next level with less effort. We focus on training you how to work smarter, not harder. We offer a wide spectrum of services that are guaranteed to meet you where you are and give you the tools *you* need to bring your message to the world, and to make a lucrative living doing so.

Remember that deciding to be patient doesn't mean that transformation needs to take a long time. Your personal transformation can happen in a moment, even if it takes some time for the rest of your life to catch up with you. Decide that instead of taking a year to change, you will change right now. Pack in forty years of experience in one year by committing to master the skills and mindset necessary to live your ideal lifestyle. Go back through the exercises I've given you in the book and start taking transformative action right now. If you haven't done the exercises, do them. If you've done them, take them to the next level and jump. If you know you need to talk to twenty people to get to your first $2,000 sale, you could do that over six months, or you can decide to do that in a week. Gain momentum, then accelerate. Decide to be a 100 percenter and do whatever it takes to get results faster. Be patient during the gestation period, trusting that results are guaranteed on the path of action.

Passion and Repetition

Remember this formula for success: Passion + Repetition + Proven Strategies = Exponential Success. If you apply any of these proven strategies I've shared with you and success doesn't come, it's not working for only one of two reasons: either you don't have enough passion, or you didn't repeat the strategy enough times. I guarantee that you're going to run into both tests repeatedly as you position yourself to evolve. Be ready for that and decide now that you will not be defeated. If something isn't working, recalibrate and try again. When you hit a wall, recognize that the wall is only a smoke screen inside your own mind. Clear the baggage in order to reignite your passion, and keep moving. There is a threshold to your comfort zone and it's going to take massive, intentional action to break through that. Inspiration and solutions come readily to those in motion. There is always a way through, and there is always a finite number of steps between where you are and where you want to be. The more you take action, the smaller the gap between you and the threshold to your success will be. Increase your energy, increase your results. $E=mc^2$.

So, commit to the passion by deciding to repeat the processes that generate the passion. Commit to the repetition by making the decision to continue to move even when it's uncomfortable.

And above all—don't wait for things to be perfect before you move.

Run Toward it!

The thing I see that most often keeps people stuck is feeling like they need everything to be perfect before they get out there and get started. It's like this:

As a mentor and coach, I often meet people who say, "Yes, I want to get my message out—I *have* to do that." So, they enlist in the race and decide they're going to do this. They pay the money to get into the game. They are on the starting line, getting into position, when suddenly they remember they don't have a website. It's like looking at their shoes and saying, "You know what, these shoes just aren't right for this race. If I had the right shoes, then I'd be ready to run this race." So, they get off the start line and go get a website.

Then they come to the start line and they begin to stretch and get pumped. They look ahead, visualizing their goals—the

147

finish line—but just as they're moving into position, they look down again and realize their jersey is all wrong. "Oh, no! I don't have business cards! And I can't be ready until I've fine-tuned my message!" They get off the start line again, and they go order cards, and they go think about their message and make sure it's perfect and that it's the right one. Then they come back to the start line again. But they're tired.

They say, "This race is tiring me out. I just need a break. I've been at this so long, and I haven't seen any results!" So, they get off the start line *again*, and say, "I just need to hire a coach to help me get through this."

So, the coach comes in, makes a quick assessment, and then says the obvious. "In order to get what you want, **you've got to run the freaking race**! Get off the start line!"

The runner says, "I'm trying! I've been running so long already. I need a website, I need cards, I need a process, I need this, and that, and everything else—it all needs to be perfect so that I can be successful and achieve all of my dreams."

However, if the coach they've hired is any good, he's just going to say, "All you need is your message, and you already have that. You already know your story. Why do you have to get off the start line in order to figure it out? You've lived it your whole life. It's time to take a step forward. Go practice the skill set of enrolling clients... *Now.*"

That first step represents one enrollment conversation with someone. So, they take one step and find someone to share their offer with. They share their stories and look for people who resonate with what they're sharing. They nervously practice. But guess what? That first time they step off the start line, they twist their ankle—the person they're talking to rejects them. So, they get out of the race again.

"I ran that race! I put in so much time, and it didn't work!"

The coach just looks at them and says, "How many steps did you take? How many people did you talk to?"

"Uh.... One."

Even if the answer is four or five steps—four or five conversations—the coach just looks at them and says, "And you expect to be at the finish line by now? No, you've got to keep moving and do what it takes. Take *fifteen* steps."

Go talk to fifteen different people to practice your pre-strategy session. Out of those fifteen people, you're guaranteed to get one or two who are going to enroll with you because you've talked to enough people at that point for the numbers to start working for you. You've fumbled and you've messed up, but you kept getting up and running the race. After the tenth or fifteenth person, you get your first enrollment for a couple grand, and all of a sudden, you're excited, wondering if you can duplicate that. You keep going and suddenly, what looked impossible is now possible because you now have the necessary skill sets, and you're mastering the necessary emotions to make it a reality.

Remember, the definition of the Enrollment Effect is to gain the skills and master the emotions necessary to live your vision, purpose, and dreams with joy while deciding you will do everything it takes to overcome any obstacle standing in your way. As you do that, you'll be able to go out and duplicate the Enrollment Effect by helping others do the same. I promise that as you come to recognize that the true effect you're striving for is to make sure every conversation you have is an authentic one, whether they enroll or not, you will satisfy your mission just by being in the business of uplifting people and the whole planet.

Then, it becomes a beautiful race to run.

About the Author

Tyler J. Watson is the founder and president of The Freedom Catalyst, which has produced several powerful, proven products in the coaching and speaking industry that help clients crystallize their message and create multiple streams of income doing what they love. These products are defined by his unique set of strategies for mastering relationships, financial growth, and emotional breakthroughs. Industry-peers have called him "a mix between Houdini and Tony Robbins" because of his trademark ability to help others significantly increase performance in their business and personal life, and step into a place of transformation and passion.

He has spent over 30,000 hours in personal one-on-one coaching sessions and is a sought-after international speaker and coach who has shared the stage with greats such as Sharon Lechter, Dan Clark, Richard Paul Evans, Tim Ralston, Maria Whalen, Ted McGrath, David Fagan, and Ann Washburn.

His international movement, *the Global Enrollment Effect*, aims to help individuals all across the world dedicate their lives to their unique purpose that will bring them the highest fulfillment while serving humanity to the fullest. His life's mission is to help entrepreneurs, coaches, speakers, and sales professionals live the life they have always dreamed about but never knew how to create. Above all, he is a passionate father and husband who actively serves in his community. He practices what he preaches and aims to transform the planet one person at a time, beginning in his own home.